THE TRUE REPUBLICAN
or AMERICAN WHIG

"THE TRUTH OUR GUIDE—THE PUBLIC GOOD OUR END"

1809 CE

Wilmington
North Carolina
USA

Newspaper Transcription
with
Historical and Genealogical Notes

Joseph E. Waters Sheppard

HERITAGE BOOKS
2008

HERITAGE BOOKS
AN IMPRINT OF HERITAGE BOOKS, INC.

Books, CDs, and more—Worldwide

For our listing of thousands of titles see our website
at
www.HeritageBooks.com

Published 2008 by
HERITAGE BOOKS, INC.
Publishing Division
100 Railroad Ave. #104
Westminster, Maryland 21157

Copyright © 2008 Joseph E. Waters Sheppard

All rights reserved. No part of this book may be reproduced or transmitted in any form or by any means, electronic or mechanical, including photocopying, recording or by any information storage and retrieval system without written permission from the author, except for the inclusion of brief quotations in a review.

International Standard Book Numbers
Paperbound: 978-0-7884-4593-4
Clothbound: 978-0-7884-7690-7

THE TRUE REPUBLICAN,
OR AMERICAN WHIG.
"The Truth our Guide – The Public Good our End."

1809 CE
Wilmington, North Carolina, USA

Newspaper transcription with historical and genealogical notes
By Joseph E. Waters Sheppard

The number and geographical distribution of newspapers grew rapidly during the United States Early National Era, 1784–1820. In 1800 there were roughly 175; by 1810 there were three hundred and sixty-six newspapers. The Democratic-Republican Party, founded by Thomas Jefferson and James Madison as the Republican Party in 1792, was the dominant political party in the United States from 1800 until the 1820s. The party and its members identified themselves as the Republican Party (not related to the present-day Republican Party) or Jeffersonian, Democratic-Republicans, less frequently Democrats, and combinations of these (*Jeffersonian Republicans*). The United States presidential election of 1800 sometimes referred to as the "Revolution of 1800," was a realigning election in which Thomas Jefferson and his running-mate, Aaron Burr, defeated incumbent President John Adams. In the United States presidential election of 1808, the (Democratic) Republican candidate James Madison defeated Federalist candidate Charles Cotesworth Pinckney. The elections ushered in a generation of (Democratic) Republican rule and the eventual demise of the Federalist Party. The Jeffersonian Republican press grew from the material benefit of patronage when the Republicans took control of the government. The Republican Party was especially effective in building a network of newspapers in major cities to broadcast its statements and editorialize in its favor. The newspapers continued as primarily party organs, though they gradually gained poise and attained a degree of literary excellence and professional dignity.

The True Republican or American Whig {*TR*} was a weekly Tuesday newspaper established in Wilmington, North Carolina. The premier edition was printed on 3 January 1809. The newspaper's editors were Thomas Watson (1786-1870) and Salmon Hall (1771-1840). Both men were residents of New Bern, North Carolina. Mr. Watson, an emigrant from Ireland, was also the printer of a weekly newspaper in New Bern titled *The Herald* which changed to the *True Republican and Newbern Weekly Advertiser* in March 1810. In 1812, Watson was appointed postmaster of New Bern, a position he held until 1837. Watson and his immediate family moved to St. Louis, Missouri. They are mentioned in the Federal Census population schedules. Thomas Watson was known for his robust editorial skirmishes with other newspaper's editors, such as, William Soranzo Hasell (1781-1815) who published *The Wilmington Gazette*. Salmon Hall, a native of Connecticut, was a bookseller by trade and co-edited the *TR* until March of 1809. He was replaced by John Ramsey (died 1825) who co-edited with Watson until late July. The newspaper discontinued soon after the early November issue. Wilmington citizens were given an account of national and international news through the *TR*. Information pertaining to daily needs and events in Wilmington and nearby towns were made known, for example, reports of vessels entering port or houses for rent. Some marriage and death notices that appear in the *TR* are missing from vital civic or religious records. Transcriptions or other forms of abstraction from the *TR* were overlooked in other genealogical and historical compiled sources. The newspapers help shape our understanding of life in that year, a time described as a *"Rip Van Winkle"* period in the Wilmington community's story. Enjoy.

HOW TO USE THIS BOOK

The author's intention is to stop and examine the period more closely. He recommends viewing the original source material. *The True Republican or American Whig*, a four (4) page weekly newspaper, was read from microfilm housed in the Special Collections Department of the New Hanover County Public Library, Wilmington, North Carolina. The American Antiquarian Society in Worcester, Massachusetts owns the originals. All issues are missing except for the following of 1809: 3, 10, 17, and 24 January; 14, 21, and 28 February; 7, 14, and 21 March; 18 April; 2, 9, 16, and 23 May; 6 and 20 June; 4 July; and 7 November. The newspaper abstractions are arranged chronologically. Each entry has an identification number beginning with 001. The newspaper stories or advertisements are copied in full or partial abstraction. The information was copied as it is represented in print by font size, capitalization or *font* style. First and last family names are in **bold**. The author cited the source following each notation by the title of the newspaper in *italics*, the volume and number [Vol. No.], town and state, day of publication, and the page and column numbers. Some newspaper notices are repeated in successive issues. Each was cited so as to know how many times it was printed. Example:

014. WANTED IMMEDIATELY, Ten or Twelve good Jon Carpenters, TO whom generous wages will be given for three or four Months. Apply at this Office. January 3, 1809. Apply to **A. F. MACNEILL** & Co. *The True Republican or American Whig* [Vol. 1. No. 1] Wilmington, NC, Tuesday, 3 January 1809, page 3, column 3. *The True Republican or American Whig* [Vol. 1. No. 2] Wilmington, NC, Tuesday, 10 January 1809, page 3, column 4. *The True Republican or American Whig* [Vol. 1. No. 3] Wilmington, NC, Tuesday, 17 January 1809, page 4, column 4. *The True Republican or American Whig* [Vol. 1. No. 4] Wilmington, NC, Tuesday, 24 January 1809, page 3, column 4. *The True Republican or American Whig* [Vol. 1. No. 7] Wilmington, NC, Tuesday, 14 February 1809, page 4, column 3.

In some instances, the author uses his own knowledge of world history or footnotes additional historical data that concerns the persons or events described in the newspaper articles or he inserts the information in brackets [ ]. The index begins on page 70. The names and subjects are indexed by the abstract's identification number, for example, 002 or *footnote* 3 (page 8). Also included in this transcription for comparison study is *The Wilmington Gazette* {*WG*} of 1809. Three issues of the *WG* survive from 1809: 3 January; 14 March; and 23 May. The *WG* was first issued in 1796 and was published by William S. Hasell from 1807 through 1815.

ACKNOWLEDGEMENTS

Special thank you to historians Beverly Tetterton-Opheim and James Michael Whaley and Ann Hewlett Hutteman all of Wilmington, North Carolina. Also thanks to the North Carolina Collection, New Hanover County Public Library and Victor T. Jones, Local History and Genealogy Librarian, Craven County Public Library, New Bern, North Carolina and the staff at the St. Louis County Public Library, St. Louis, Missouri.

THE TRUE REPUBLICAN

001. *MR. GILES'* [1] *SPEECH,* Delivered in Senate of the United States, on Thursday, 24th November, 1808, on the resolution of Mr. **Hillhouse**, to repeal the Embargo Laws [2] *. . . continued.* The True Republican or American Whig [Vol. 1. No. 1] Wilmington, NC, Tuesday, 3 January 1809, page 1, column 1 – page 2, column 3.

002. EXTRACT OF A LETTER *From a gentleman at Liverpool, to his friend in Philadelphia, dated Liverpool 22d October, 1808.* "The continuance of the embargo in the U.S. preventing all opportunities of shipments of produce from thence, we have not of late thought it necessary to continue our advices of the state of our market to the generality of our friends: as an opinion is now, however entertained by many, that the embargo will be taken off before the end of the year, we avail ourselves of the present opportunities of stating the prices of American produce, as well as prospects for it in our market . . . *continued. The True Republican or American Whig* [Vol. 1. No. 1] Wilmington, NC, Tuesday, 3 January 1809, page 2, columns 3 & 4.

003. Congress. SENATE – December 17. The bill to authorize and require the President of the United States to arm, man and fit out for immediate service all the public ships of war, vessels and gunboats of the United States, was read the third time and passed. The bill appropriates 400,000 dollars. The bill making further provision for enforcing the embargo was read the third time: when a debate commenced on its passage. Mr. **Goodrich** spoke at length against the bill, when the Senate adjourned, without taking the question. *The True Republican or American Whig* [Vol. 1. No. 1] Wilmington, NC, Tuesday, 3 January 1809, page 2, column 4.

004. HOUSE OF REPRESENTATIVES. Friday, December 16. REPORT ON FINANCES. The Speaker laid before the House the annual report of the Secretary of the Treasury. The report having been read. Mr. **Randolph** said, as this was an extremely interesting report, he hoped means would be taken for expediting the printing and that more than the ordinary number would be printed. On motion of Mr. **G. W. Campbell**, 2000 copies of the report and the usual number of the documents accompanying it, were ordered to be printed. . . *continued. The True Republican or American Whig* [Vol. 1. No. 1] Wilmington, NC, Tuesday, 3 January 1809, page 3, columns 1 & 2.

005. The True Republican. WILMINGTON, Tuesday, January 3, 1809. In soliciting the patronage of the public to the support of this paper, we conceive it to be a duty to declare the principles on which it is predicted, and the political course which shall distinguish our Editorial career. . . *continued. The True Republican or American Whig* [Vol. 1. No. 1] Wilmington, NC, Tuesday, 3 January 1809, page 3, column 2.

---

[1] **William Branch Giles** (1762-1830), a statesman elected from Virginia to Congress in 1790 and then again in 1801 and 1804. He was elected Governor of Virginia in 1827. *North-Carolina Journal* (Fayetteville, NC), Vol. 5, No. 241, 22 December 1830, page 1.

[2] EMBARGO OF 1807: This law was passed in December 1807 over Federalist opposition, and prohibited United States vessels from trading with European nations during the Napoleonic War. The Embargo Act was in response to the restrictive measure imposed on American neutrality by France and Britain, who where at war with each other. To pressure the nations to respect the neutral rights of the United States and to demonstrate the value of trade with the United States, Jefferson imposed the embargo instead of open warfare. Non-Intercourse Act: The Non-Intercourse Act of 1 March 1809, repealed the Embargo Act, and reactivated American commerce with all countries except the warring French and the British. The United States also agreed to resume trade with the first nation of the two, who would cease violating neutral rights, pressuring the needs for American goods.

006. The True Republican will appear on a new Type by the first of April, the Editors having ordered a supply from Philadelphia. *The True Republican or American Whig* [Vol. 1. No. 1] Wilmington, NC, Tuesday, 3 January 1809, page 3, column 3.

007. Bank of Cape Fear. RESOLVED. That no note will be discounted at this Bank or its agencies unless made and endorsed after the 1st of January 1809. Provided that this resolution shall not extend to Notes offered for collection although dated pervious to the 1st of January 1809. By order of the Directors. **JOHN HOGG**, *Cashier*. Jan. 3. *The Wilmington Gazette* [Number 626. 13th Year] Wilmington, NC, Tuesday, 3 January 1809, page 2, column 4.

008. At an election held yesterday for Directors of the Bank of Cape Fear, the following gentlemen were duly elected – **Joshua G. Wright, John London, George Hooper, William Campbell, Aaron Lazarus, John Bradley, William Giles, David Anderson, Duncan M'Learan, John M'Millan,** and **Robert Mitchell**. After which, the Directors proceeded to the choice of President for the ensuing year when **Joshua G. Wright**, Esq., was elected. *The True Republican or American Whig* [Vol. 1. No. 1] Wilmington, NC, Tuesday, 3 January 1809, page 3, column 3. Also printed in *The Wilmington Gazette* [Number 626. 13th Year] Wilmington, NC, Tuesday, 3 January 1809, page 3, column 1.

009. TUESDAY, January 3, 1809. We understand that Major General **Smith** has received orders from the Commander in Chief, to immediately organize the quota to be raised for his division of the Militia. – We are informed that Mr. **H. Kelly**, Agent for this State, has received orders to charter a suitable vessel to transport immediately one company of 60 men to New Orleans. *The Wilmington Gazette* [Number 626. 13th Year] Wilmington, NC, Tuesday, 3 January 1809, page 3, column 1.

010. Married. On Sunday evening last, by **Hanson Kelly**, Esq., Capt. **James T. Gibson** of the English Schooner[3] Dolphin to Mrs. **Eleanor Creighton**, of this place. *The True Republican or American Whig* [Vol. 1. No. 1] Wilmington, NC, Tuesday, 3 January 1809, page 3, column 3. Also printed in *The Wilmington Gazette* [Number 626. 13th Year] Wilmington, NC, Tuesday, 3 January 1809, page 3, column 4.

011. Communication. Died lately, in Jamaica, Mrs. **Muter**, relict of Mr. **Robert Muter**, merchant, formerly a resident of this town.[4] *The Wilmington Gazette* [Number 626. 13th Year] Wilmington, NC, Tuesday, 3 January 1809, page 3, column 4.

012. PORT OF WILMINGTON. ENTERED. Dec. 27. Sch'r Enterprize, **Joyce**, Newbern. 28. Issabella, **Bourne**, Boston. Do. Henry Dennison, **Allen**, New York. 30. Trio, **Bailey**, Boston. 31. Brig[5] Alexis, **Livingston**, Liverpool. Jan. 2. Ship Mary, **Warton**, New York. Do. Sloop[6] Patty

---

[3] A **schooner** is a type of sailing vessel characterized by the use of fore-and-aft sails on two or more masts. Schooners were first used by the Dutch in the 16th or 17th century, and further developed in North America from the time of the American Revolution.

[4] **Margaret Muter**, sometimes Meeter, is mentioned as wife in **Robert Muter**'s will, probated in July 1806 (New Hanover County Will Book AB, page 95.) Four of the **Muter**'s children died and were interred in Saint James Cemetery at Market and Fourth streets, Wilmington, North Carolina, between the years 1788 and 1793. The gravestone has printed on it, "The offspring of Robert and Margaret **Muter**, formerly of Portsmouth, Virginia." Mrs. **Muter**'s will was probated in May 1810 (NHC Will Book AB, page 132.)

[5] In nautical terms, a **brig** is a vessel of 23-50 m length (75 and 165 feet) with two square-rigged masts, and tonnage weight up to 480. During the Age of Sail, brigs were seen as fast and maneuverable with speeds up to 11 knots and were used as both naval war ships and merchant ships. While their use stretches back before the 1600s the most famous period of the brig was during the 1800s when they were involved in famous naval battles. Because they required a

and Lydia, **Sutton**, Charleston. Do. Sch'r Rebecca, **West**, Boston. Do. Isabella, **Barkman**, Matanzas. CLEARED. Dec. 29. Sch'r Betty, **Holmes**, Boston. 30. Enterprize, **Joyce**, Newbern. Jan. 2. Brig Portland, **Crabtree**, Philad. *The True Republican or American Whig* [Vol. 1. No. 1] Wilmington, NC, Tuesday, 3 January 1809, page 3, column 3. Also printed in *The Wilmington Gazette* [Number 626. 13th Year] Wilmington, NC, Tuesday, 3 January 1809, page 3, column 4.

013. DESERTER. **JOHN BROWN**, from the United States Gun-Boat[7] No. 7. – He is well known about Town and lived last year, I am informed, at **John Hill**'s Esq., said deserter is from Rhode Island. He took with him sundry new cloaths. – A reward of Twenty Dollars will be given for his apprehension if out of State, and delivered to any officer in the Naval Service of the U. States, or ten Dollars if taken within 20 miles of Wilmington and secured in the County Jail so that I get him again. All necessary expenses will be paid. **T. N. GAUTIER**. January 3, 1809. *The True Republican or American Whig* [Vol. 1. No. 1] Wilmington, NC, Tuesday, 3 January 1809, page 3, column 3. *The True Republican or American Whig* [Vol. 1. No. 2] Wilmington, NC, Tuesday, 10 January 1809, page 3, column 3. *The True Republican or American Whig* [Vol. 1. No. 3] Wilmington, NC, Tuesday, 17 January 1809, page 4, column 3. *The True Republican or American Whig* [Vol. 1. No. 4] Wilmington, NC, Tuesday, 24 January 1809, page 4, column 4.

014. WANTED IMMEDIATELY, Ten or Twelve good Jon Carpenters, TO whom generous wages will be given for three or four Months. Apply at this Office. January 3, 1809. Apply to **A. F. MACNEILL** & Co. *The True Republican or American Whig* [Vol. 1. No. 1] Wilmington, NC, Tuesday, 3 January 1809, page 3, column 3. *The True Republican or American Whig* [Vol. 1. No. 2] Wilmington, NC, Tuesday, 10 January 1809, page 3, column 4. *The True Republican or American Whig* [Vol. 1. No. 3] Wilmington, NC, Tuesday, 17 January 1809, page 4, column 4. *The True Republican or American Whig* [Vol. 1. No. 4] Wilmington, NC, Tuesday, 24 January 1809, page 3, column 4. *The True Republican or American Whig* [Vol. 1. No. 7] Wilmington, NC, Tuesday, 14 February 1809, page 4, column 3.

015. WILMINGTON PRICES CURRENT. January 3d, 1809. [The actual article for *Wilmington Prices Current* prints the items for sale in top to bottom style with the D (dollar) and C (cents) horizontal from the sale item.] Tobacco, cwt. 3.50. Pork, bl. 8 to 9 dollars. Flour, bl. 6 dollars. Tar, bl. 1.12 to 1.25. Turpentine, bl. 2 to 2.25. Rice, cwt. 2 dollars. Rum, 4th proof, 1.50. Sugar brown, 11 to 13 dollars, Coffee, 35 cents. Molasses, 56 cents. Salt, 1 dollar. Corn, bush, 50 cents. Peas, bush 50 cents. Bacon, Hams & Shoulders, 8 to 9 dollars. Lard, lb. 10 cents. Lumber, 1x1x4 Inch Boards, 8 to 8.5' dollars. Lumber Scantling, no sale. Staves, W. O. Hhds 1000, 15 to 18 dollars. Staves, R. O. do, 7 to 8

---

relatively large crew of 12 to 16 and the difficulty of sailing into the wind (a trait common to all square-rigged ships), brigs were phased out of use by the arrival of the steamboat. They are not to be confused with a brigantine which has different rigging.

[6] A **sloop** (From Dutch *sloep*) in sailing, is a vessel with a fore-and-aft rig. A sloop carries a single mast stepped farther forward than that of a cutter. The sloop's fore-triangle is smaller than a cutter's. As such, the sloop usually bends only one headsail, though this distinction is not definitive. A cutter rig generally carries multiple headsails, however sloops such as the Friendship Sloop carry more than one headsail and are properly designated a sloop and not a cutter. Ultimately position of the mast is the most important factor.

[7] A **gunboat** is literally a boat carrying one or more guns. The term is rather broad, and the usual connotation has changed over the years. In the Age of Sail, a gunboat was usually a small undecked vessel carrying a single smoothbore cannon in the bow. A gunboat could carry one or two masts or be oar-powered only, but the single-masted version of about 50 ft length was most typical. Some types of gunboats carried two cannons, or else mounted a number of swivel guns on the railings.

dollars. Staves, W. O. do. Bls. 75 cents. *The True Republican or American Whig* [Vol. 1. No. 1] Wilmington, NC, Tuesday, 3 January 1809, page 3, column 4.

016. Wanted to Charter, FOR PHILADELPHIA; ONE or two Vessels, drawing not more than 11 feet water when loaded. Apply to **I. FLEMING**. Who offers For Sale, 3500 Bushels Turks Island SALT. January 3d, 1809. *The True Republican or American Whig* [Vol. 1. No. 1] Wilmington, NC, Tuesday, 3 January 1809, page 3, column 4. *The True Republican or American Whig* [Vol. 1. No. 2] Wilmington, NC, Tuesday, 10 January 1809, page 3, column 4. *The True Republican or American Whig* [Vol. 1. No. 3] Wilmington, NC, Tuesday, 17 January 1809, page 4, column 4. *The True Republican or American Whig* [Vol. 1. No. 7] Wilmington, NC, Tuesday, 14 February 1809, page 4, column 4.

017. NOTICE. ANY PERSONS willing to contract for building a Court House at Smithville,[8] are desired to send sealed proposals to the Subscriber, before the 25th day of January 1809; on the following principles: - 1st to be built altogether of Brick 40 by 30, from out to out, foundation, if of Stone, two feet thick, if of Brick, two feet and a half thick, one foot under and one above ground – first Story two brick thick, ten feet high in the clear, altogether Brick. – Second Story, one Brick and a half thick, twelve feet in the clear, -- Roof and finishing of the whole familiar, at least equal to the Court-House in Wilmington, except the steps which are to be made substantially & of handsome form on the outside wall secured -- . . . **ALEXANDER DUNN** One of the Board of Commissioners and Treasurer. Smithville, Dec. 30, 1808. *The True Republican or American Whig* [Vol. 1. No. 1] Wilmington, NC, Tuesday, 3 January 1809, page 3, column 4. *The True Republican or American Whig* [Vol. 1. No. 2] Wilmington, NC, Tuesday, 10 January 1809, page 3, column 3. *The True Republican or American Whig* [Vol. 1. No. 3] Wilmington, NC, Tuesday, 17 January 1809, page 4, column 3.

018. **WILLIAM DICK**, At the Sign of the SPREAD EAGLE, Has removed from Second to First Street, a few doors north of the Bank, where his HOTEL is prepared as heretofore; to receive such company, transient or permanent as may honor him with their custom. The charges remain the same, while the change of place will doubtless render it a more agreeable stand for societies or clubs to meet at, or residence to those who may be inclined to board there. Jan. 3. *The True Republican or American Whig* [Vol. 1. No. 1] Wilmington, NC, Tuesday, 3 January 1809, page 3, column 4. *The True Republican or American Whig* [Vol. 1. No. 2] Wilmington, NC, Tuesday, 10 January 1809, page 3, column 3. *The True Republican or American Whig* [Vol. 1. No. 3] Wilmington, NC, Tuesday, 17 January 1809, page 4, column 3. *The True Republican or American Whig* [Vol. 1. No. 4] Wilmington, NC, Tuesday, 24 January 1809, page 4, column 4. *The True Republican or American Whig* [Vol. 1. No. 7] Wilmington, NC, Tuesday, 14 February 1809, page 4, column 3. *The True Republican or American Whig* [Vol. 1. No. 8] Wilmington, NC, Tuesday, 21 February 1809, page 4, column 4 *The True Republican or American Whig* [Vol. 1. No. 9] Wilmington, NC, Tuesday, 28 February 1809, page 4, column 4. *The True Republican or American Whig* [Vol. 1. No. 11] Wilmington, NC, Tuesday, 14 March 1809, page 4, column 2. *The Wilmington Gazette* [Number 636. 13th Year] Wilmington, NC, Tuesday, 14 March 1809, page 2, column 4. *The True Republican or American Whig* [Vol. 1. No. 12] Wilmington, NC, Tuesday, 21 March 1809, page 2, column 4.

019. FOR RENT – OR SALE, THE HOUSE & LOT. Now occupied by Mr. **James Usher**, on the Hill, adjoining **George W. B. Burgwin**, Esq. Possession will be given immediately. For further information enquire of **JOHN USHER**. January 3, 1809. *The True Republican or American Whig* [Vol. 1. No. 1] Wilmington, NC, Tuesday, 3 January 1809, page 3, column 4. *The True Republican or American Whig* [Vol. 1. No. 2] Wilmington, NC, Tuesday, 10 January 1809, page 3, column 4. *The True Republican or American Whig* [Vol. 1. No. 3] Wilmington, NC, Tuesday, 17 January 1809, page 4, column 4.

020. BRICKS FOR SALE. From 1 to 400,000 Bricks may be purchased for Cash, or six months Credit. Apply to **A. F. MACNEILL**. January 3, 1809. *The True Republican or American Whig* [Vol. 1. No. 1] Wilmington, NC, Tuesday, 3 January 1809, page 3, column 4. *The True Republican or American Whig* [Vol. 1. No. 2] Wilmington, NC, Tuesday, 10 January 1809, page 3, column 4. *The True Republican or American Whig* [Vol. 1. No. 3] Wilmington, NC, Tuesday, 17 January 1809, page 4, column 4.

---

[8] Smithville, North Carolina, developed by 1792 and was named for Gen. **Benjamin Smith** (1751-1826). Name changed to Southport in 1889 because it was the most southerly seaport in the state.

021. For sale at this office, **Watson & Hall**'s ALMANACK for 1809. *The True Republican or American Whig* [Vol. 1. No. 1] Wilmington, NC, Tuesday, 3 January 1809, page 3, column 4.

022. NEW YEAR'S REFLECTIONS, Once more the Globe its annual course has run, *continued*. *The True Republican or American Whig* [Vol. 1. No. 1] Wilmington, NC, Tuesday, 3 January 1809, page 4, column 1.

023. PENNSYLVANIA LEGISLATURE. At 12 o'clock this day (Dec. 8) the Governor, accompanied by the officers of government entered the chamber of the House of Representatives, and delivered the following SPEECH: *continued*. [Signed by] **THOMAS M'KEAN**. Lancaster Dec. 8, 1808. *The True Republican or American Whig* [Vol. 1. No. 1] Wilmington, NC, Tuesday, 3 January 1809, page 4, cols. 2-4.

024. PUBLISHED WEEKLY BY **THOMAS WATSON & SALMON HALL**,[9] On Second, Near Market Street, At three Dollars per annum, in advance, or three Dollars and fifty Cents, if not paid within the year. *The True Republican or American Whig* [Vol. 1. No. 1] Wilmington, NC, Tuesday, 3 January 1809, page 4, column 4.

025. Wilmington, NC. PRINTED AND PUBLISHED by **William S. Hasell**[10] At three Dollars a year, payable in advance, or Four Dollars if not paid within the first Six months. *The Wilmington Gazette* [Number 626. 13th Year] Wilmington, NC, Tuesday, 3 January 1809, page 4, column 4.

026. SENATE OF THE UNITED STATES. EMBARGO DEBATE. MR. **GILES**' SPEECH, [Continued] But, Sir, I and mention another circumstance, which may be some alleviation to the farmer, for the difference in the price of his surplus plenty now, and in ordinary times. . .
continued. *The True Republican or American Whig* [Vol. 1. No. 2] Wilmington, NC, Tuesday, 10 January 1809, page 1, column 1 – page 2, column 1. The next article I shall mention is TOBACCO. What says the Liverpool merchants respecting this article?. . . *The True Republican or American Whig* [Vol. 1. No. 3] Wilmington, NC, Tuesday, 17 January 1809, page 1, column 1 – page 2, column 2. The gentleman from Connecticut (Mr. **Hillhouse**) says that the embargo is submission . . . *The True Republican or American Whig* [Vol. 1. No. 4] Wilmington, NC, Tuesday, 24 January 1809, page 1, column 1 – page 2, column. 2.

027. BRITISH INFLUENCE. The following able and perspicuous exhibition of the great question, we copy with an ardent and entire accordance with the unanswerable sentiments it so will expresses. FROM THE BALTIMORE EVENING POST. In all the debates and proceedings of the representatives of the people, in congress assembled, we do not hear a single, solitary

---

[9] DIED. In Newbern on the 28th, ult. Mr. **Salmon Hall**, in the 69th year of his age, a native of Connecticut. *Wilmington Weekly Chronicle*, Wilmington, NC, Wednesday, 10 June 1840, Vol. II No. 56, page 3, column 4. Deaths. In Newbern, on the 28th instant, after a protracted illness, which he bore with the meek submission of a good man, Mr. **SALMON HALL**, bookseller, in the 69th year of his age. The *Fayetteville Observer*, Fayetteville, NC, Wednesday, 10 June 1840, page 3, column 5.

[10] Notice. IS hereby given of the death of **William S. Hasell** Esq., late of Wilmington, and that at November term 1815 of the County Court of Pleas and Quarter sessions in, and for the County of New Hanover, the subscriber obtained letters of Administration on the estate of the said **William S. Hasell**. All persons indebted to the said estate, are notified to make payment without delay, and those who have claims against the same to present them to the subscriber for liquidation within the time prescribed by an act of Assembly, entitled "An act to amend an act entitled an act concerning proving of Wills and granting letters of Administration, and to prevent frauds in the management of Intestate estates," otherwise this notice will be plead in law of recovery. **Wm. H. HALSEY** Adm'r. *Wilmington Gazette, Commercial and Political* [Vol. XII, 975] Wilmington, NC, Saturday, 13 January 1816, page 1, column 4.

Republican, attempting to justify the measures adopted by France to inure the rights of neutrality . . . *cont. The True Republican or American Whig* [Vol. 1. No. 2] Wilmington, NC, Tuesday, 10 January 1809, page 2, column 2 – page 3, column 1.

028. CONGRESS. HOUSE OF REPRESENTATIVES. FRIDAY, DEC. 28, 1808 [The actual date was the Thirtieth of December 1808.] Mr. **Burwell**, That is expedient that a committee be appointed to inquire into the extent to which the article of salt is, or can be supplied from, the salt establishments within the United States, and that effectual means be immediately taken to render the supply adequate to the consumption and wants of the nation . . . *continued. The True Republican or American Whig* [Vol. 1. No. 2] Wilmington, NC, Tuesday, 10 January 1809, page 2, columns 1 & 2.

029. Monday December 26, 1808. Mr. **Nelson**, from the committee on military and naval affairs, made the following report in part. Resolved. That it is expedient immediately to raise, arm, and equip fifty thousand volunteers, to serve for the term of two years . . . *continued. The True Republican or American Whig* [Vol. 1. No. 2] Wilmington, NC, Tuesday, 10 January 1809, page 2, column 2.

030. PROPOSALS, For publishing by subscription A TRANSLATION OF THE MESSIAH. In English blank verse; an Epic Poem, written originally in the German Language by, MR. **KLOPSTOCK**, So justly celebrated by the Literati of Europe, as "the Milton of Germany:" . . *cont.* S. **HALLING**, A.M. Rector of the St. James' Church, Wilmington, NC. Oct. 13, 1808. Subscriptions received at this Office.[11] *The True Republican or American Whig* [Vol. 1. No. 2] Wilmington, NC, Tuesday, 10 January 1809, page 2, column 3. *The True Republican or American Whig* [Vol. 1. No. 3] Wilmington, NC, Tuesday, 17 January 1809, page 4, column 3. *The True Republican or American Whig* [Vol. 1. No. 4] Wilmington, NC, Tuesday, 24 January 1809, page 4, column 4. *The True Republican or American Whig* [Vol. 1. No. 7] Wilmington, NC, Tuesday, 14 February 1809, page 4, column 3. *The True Republican or American Whig* [Vol. 1. No. 9] Wilmington, NC, Tuesday, 28 February 1809, page 4, column 4.

031. NOTICE. THE SUBSCRIBERS have determined to discontinue the Sale of GOODS, except for CASH. All persons indebted to them on open accounts, are desired to call and settle the same. They also request, all those indebted to them by bonds, Notes and open Accounts, which have been long due, to come forward before the 25th of March next and make payment, or confess judgment, subject to the suspension of Executions. After that day, circumstances will compel the Subscribers, however reluctantly, to institute Suits without discrimination. **GILES & BURGWIN**. Wilmington, Jan. 9, 1809. *The True Republican or American Whig* [Vol. 1. No. 2] Wilmington, NC, Tuesday, 10 January 1809, page 3, column 4. *The True Republican or American Whig* [Vol. 1. No. 3] Wilmington, NC, Tuesday, 17 January 1809, page 4, column 4. *The True Republican or American Whig* [Vol. 1. No. 4] Wilmington, NC, Tuesday, 24 January 1809, page 4, column 4. *The True Republican or American Whig* [Vol. 1. No. 7] Wilmington, NC, Tuesday, 14 February 1809, page 4, column 3. *The True Republican or American Whig* [Vol. 1. No. 8] Wilmington, NC, Tuesday, 21 February 1809, page 4, column 3. *The True Republican or American Whig* [Vol. 1. No. 9] Wilmington, NC, Tuesday, 28 February 1809, page 4, column 4. *The True Republican or American Whig* [Vol. 1. No. 10] Wilmington, NC, Tuesday, 7 March 1809, page 4, column 4. *The True Republican or American Whig* [Vol. 1. No. 11] Wilmington, NC, Tuesday, 14 March 1809, page 4, column 4. *The True Republican or American Whig* [Vol. 1. No. 12] Wilmington, NC, Tuesday, 21 March 1809, page 3, column 1 and page 4, column 4.

032. NOTICE. **THOMAS J. BEATTY** IS AUTHORIZED AS MY Agent & Attorney, to adjust and collect the debts, and settle the Business of the late Firm of **Gautier** & Co. **T. N. GAUTIER**.

---

[11] **Friedrich Gottlieb Klopstock**, born 2 July 1724, Quedlinburg, Saxony [Germany]. He died on 14 March 1803, Hamburg. German epic and lyric poet whose subjective vision marked a break with the rationalism that had dominated German literature in the early 18th century. After reading John Milton's *Paradise Lost* in the translation by the influential Swiss critic J.J. Bodmer, Klopstock chose a religious theme for the epic poem he had planned. "Klopstock, Friedrich Gottlieb." Encyclopedia Britannica. 2006. Encyclopedia Britannica Online. 31 Oct. 2006 <http://www.britannica.com/eb/article-9045766>.

December 6, 1808. *The True Republican or American Whig* [Vol. 1. No. 2] Wilmington, NC, Tuesday, 10 January 1809, page 3, column 4. *The True Republican or American Whig* [Vol. 1. No. 3] Wilmington, NC, Tuesday, 17 January 1809, page 4, column 4. *The Wilmington Gazette* [Number 636. 13th Year] Wilmington, NC, Tuesday, 14 March 1809, page 2, column 4.

033. **B. C. GILLETT**.[12] CABINET MAKER, INFORMS his former Friends and the Public in general, that he has returned to Wilmington where he has opened a CABINET WARE-HOUSE, in First Street, nearly opposite the Bank; where all kinds of Cabinet work will be done with neatness and dispatch. N. B. Gentlemen from the Country can have it put up in the safest order. Wilmington, January 9, 1809. *The True Republican or American Whig* [Vol. 1. No. 2] Wilmington, NC, Tuesday, 10 January 1809, page 3, column 4. *The True Republican or American Whig* [Vol. 1. No. 3] Wilmington, NC, Tuesday, 17 January 1809, page 4, column 4. *The True Republican or American Whig* [Vol. 1. No. 4] Wilmington, NC, Tuesday, 24 January 1809, page 4, column 3. *The True Republican or American Whig* [Vol. 1. No. 7] Wilmington, NC, Tuesday, 14 February 1809, page 4, column 3. *The True Republican or American Whig* [Vol. 1. No. 8] Wilmington, NC, Tuesday, 21 February 1809, page 4, column 4 *The True Republican or American Whig* [Vol. 1. No. 9] Wilmington, NC, Tuesday, 28 February 1809, page 4, column 4.

034. CHEAP BOOKS! **THOMAS WATSON** has just opened, and offers for Sale, at the Office of the True Republican, a general collection of choice and cheap books. A liberal deduction will be made to country Merchants & Teachers who may wish to supply themselves with School Books. SACRED MUSIC. For Sale as above . . . Jan. 10. *The True Republican or American Whig* [Vol. 1. No. 2] Wilmington, NC, Tuesday, 10 January 1809, page 3, column 4. *The True Republican or American Whig* [Vol. 1. No. 3] Wilmington, NC, Tuesday, 17 January 1809, page 4, column 4. *The True Republican or American Whig* [Vol. 1. No. 7] Wilmington, NC, Tuesday, 14 February 1809, page 4, column 4.

035. BLANK BOOKS. Merchants and others can be supplied at this office with Blank Books of every description. January 10. *The True Republican or American Whig* [Vol. 1. No. 2] Wilmington, NC, Tuesday, 10 January 1809, page 3, column 4. *The True Republican or American Whig* [Vol. 1. No. 3] Wilmington, NC, Tuesday, 17 January 1809, page 4, column 4. *The True Republican or American Whig* [Vol. 1. No. 7] Wilmington, NC, Tuesday, 14 February 1809, page 4, column 4. *The True Republican or American Whig* [Vol. 1. No. 8] Wilmington, NC, Tuesday, 21 February 1809, page 1, column 4 & page 3, column 4. *The True Republican or American Whig* [Vol. 1. No. 9] Wilmington, NC, Tuesday, 28 February 1809, page 4, column 4. *The True Republican or American Whig* [Vol. 1. No. 10] Wilmington, NC, Tuesday, 7 March 1809, page 4, column 3. *The True Republican or American Whig* [Vol. 1. No. 11] Wilmington, NC, Tuesday, 14 March 1809, page 4, column 4.

036. PUBLISHED WEEKLY BY **THOMAS WATSON & SALMON HALL**, On Second, Near Market Street, At three Dollars per annum, half in advance, or three Dollars and fifty Cents, if not paid within the year. Advertisements appearing in the TRUE REPUBLICAN will, it desired, be re-published in the NEWBERN HERALD, free of any additional charge. *The True Republican or American Whig* [Vol. 1. No. 2] Wilmington, NC, Tuesday, 10 January 1809, page 4, column 4. *The True Republican or American Whig* [Vol. 1. No. 3] Wilmington, NC, Tuesday, 17 January 1809, page 4, column 4. *The True Republican or American Whig* [Vol. 1. No. 4] Wilmington, NC, Tuesday, 24 January 1809, page 4, column 4. *The True Republican or American Whig* [Vol. 1. No. 7] Wilmington, NC, Tuesday, 14 February 1809, page 4, column 4. *The True Republican or American Whig* [Vol. 1. No. 8] Wilmington, NC, Tuesday, 21 February 1809, page 4, column 4. *The True Republican or American Whig* [Vol. 1. No. 9] Wilmington, NC, Tuesday, 28 February 1809, page 4, column 4.

037. DEBATE ON FOREIGN RELATIONS. Extracts from Mr. **Eppe**'s Speech in Reply to Mr. **Gardenier**. I shall perhaps be told as another gentleman was yesterday that my observations resemble more than slang of an ale house, than the debate of a deliberate body. . . *cont. The True Republican or American Whig* [Vol. 1. No. 3] Wilmington, NC, Tuesday, 17 January 1809, page 2, columns 2 & 3 – page 3, column 1.

---

[12] **Benjamin C. Gillett** was a native of Connecticut and died at the age of 60 in Wilmington on 27 July 1837. Burial was in St. James Cemetery. *Wilmington Advertiser* [Vol. II. No. 29] Wilmington, NC, Friday, 4 August 1837, page 3, column 4. Thanks to Ida B. Kellam, *Marriage & Death Notices in Newspapers Published in Wilmington, NC 17397-1842* (1959) and also *St. James Church Historical Records* (1965).

038. Washington City, Jan. 2. Captain **Connel**, of the Charleston packet,[13] states he left Bordeaux on the 2nd of Nov. by special permission of the emperor, through the interference of our minister for the purpose of bringing home the distressed seamen of our country belonging to vessels condemned and sequestered; . . *Continued*. *The True Republican or American Whig* [Vol. 1. No. 3] Wilmington, NC, Tuesday, 17 January 1809, page 3, columns 1 & 2.

039. Notice. THE Subscriber, being authorized to settle the business of the late Firm of *Gautier & Co.* requests all persons indebted thereto, to come forward before the 20th day of March next, and close their accounts. Those who (in consequence of the difficulty of the times) are not in a situation to make payment will be indulged by giving an acknowledgement securing interest. Those who do not comply, may rest assured, their accounts will (on the 21st same Month) be put into a Lawyers hands for collection. ALL claims against said Firm on open accounts, will be liquidated by application to. **THOS. J. BEATTY**. January 14, 1809. *The True Republican or American Whig* [Vol. 1. No. 3] Wilmington, NC, Tuesday, 17 January 1809, page 3, column 2. *The True Republican or American Whig* [Vol. 1. No. 4] Wilmington, NC, Tuesday, 24 January 1809, page 3, column 4.

040. 500 DOLLARS REWARD. LOST out of my Pocket, yesterday, a RED POCKET BOOK, Containing a considerable sum of Money, not less than THIRTEEN THOUSAND DOLLARS, all U. States Notes, except about Five Hundred Dollars of the Bank of Cape Fear, with one English Guinea. There were also therein several Invoices for Rice, Cotton, and Tobacco, signed by **Thomas N. Gautier**. Also, an Invoice for Fifty Casks Flax seed, and Forty One Casks Rice, signed by **F. Clark**; Some Amoskeag Lottery Tickets, with other Papers bearing date in Boston, having my name therein. Any person delivering said Book with the contents to me, or **Thomas N. Gautier**, in Wilmington, shall receive the above reward, and no questions asked. **JAMES WHITE**. N.B. Among the United States Notes were three Notes of one Thousand Dollars each – four of Five Hundred – balance, One Hundred – Cape Fear Notes, from Fifty Dollars downwards. One of the One Thousand Dollar Notes is endorsed by **Thomas C. Armory**, & Co. Wilmington, N.C. Jan. 12, 1809. *The True Republican or American Whig* [Vol. 1. No. 3] Wilmington, NC, Tuesday, 17 January 1809, page 3, column 3. *The True Republican or American Whig* [Vol. 1. No. 4] Wilmington, NC, Tuesday, 24 January 1809, page 2, column 4.

041. WILMINGTON, TUESDAY, JANUARY 17, 1809. Gentleman holding subscription papers for the True Republican are particularly requested to return such names as have been received, that the paper may be early addressed to its perspective patrons.

The following propositions, made by the Emperor of Russia and of France to Great Britain, were received by the Editor of the *Washington Monitor* from his correspondent at Bordeaux, . . . 1st. Hanover to be restored to G. Britain. 2$^{nd.}$ Brunswick to be restored to the heirs of the Duke . . . 6th. Joseph Napoleon to become King of Spain and the Indies.

The following extract of a letter from two of the most respectable citizens of Tennessee justly portrays the sentiments of the people of that state. . . .

Stick to the EMBARGO! The ship Ophelia, Captain **Dunner**, from Bristol, (E) for New York, with a valuable cargo of hardware was met at sea by a French ship of war and burnt!

The brig George, Captain **Douglas** from New London for St. Lucia, was captured by the French, carried into Guadeloupe, and condemned. *The True Republican or American Whig* [Vol. 1. No. 3] Wilmington, NC, Tuesday, 17 January 1809, page 3, column 3.

042. Mr. **Key**, one of the delectable representatives from Maryland in Congress of the United States, in a late speech, talked about the year *Seventeen Hundred* and *Seventy Six*. Where was he

---

[13] A **packet** ship is a vessel employed to carry Post Office mail packets to and from British colonies and outposts. The captains were generally also able to carry bullion, private goods, and passengers. The ships were usually lightly armed and relied on speed for their security.

in *this* year? What did he do during the Revolutionary War? He took up arms against his country, and became a pensioned slave to the British government; the emolument of his turpitude it is believed he continues to enjoy. Yet he is representative of the people in an American Congress.[14] *The True Republican or American Whig* [Vol. 1. No. 3] Wilmington, NC, Tuesday, 17 January 1809, page 3, column 4.

043. FROM THE *SALEM REGISTER*. The Republicans of North Salem, [Massachusetts] on the 22d inst (the anniversary of the laying the embargo), celebrated the day with a spirit which does them honor as friends of their country . . .

The communication promised in our last, being at present in the hands of Mr. **Hasell** we are not enabled to publish it in today's paper.

No northern papers were received by the STAGE on Sunday evening. *The True Republican or American Whig* [Vol. 1. No. 3] Wilmington, NC, Tuesday, 17 January 1809, page 3, column 4.

044. TO BE HIRED, Several NEGROES, Male and Female, fit for House Servants. Apply to **I. FLEMING**. January 17. *The True Republican or American Whig* [Vol. 1. No. 3] Wilmington, NC, Tuesday, 17 January 1809, page 3, column 4. *The True Republican or American Whig* [Vol. 1. No. 4] Wilmington, NC, Tuesday, 24 January 1809, page 3, column 4.

045. PORT OF WILMINGTON. ENTERED. Jan. 10. Sloop George, **Denning**, Charleston. 12. Sloop Patty, **McLean**, Ditto. CLEARED. Jan. 10. Snow Fanny, **Harkin**, Gloucester, Massachusetts. 12. Sloop Patty, **McLean**, Charleston. Sch'r Eliza Tice, **Carman**, Wilmington, Delaware. Brig Lydia, **Crabtree**, Boston. 13. Argus, **Hallowell**, Providence. Rhode Island. *The True Republican or American Whig* [Vol. 1. No. 3] Wilmington, NC, Tuesday, 17 January 1809, page 3, column 4.

046. PRICES CURRENT. WILMINGTON, JANUARY 17, 1809.

Merchandize	quan rated	from D	C.	to D	C.
Bacon,	*Lb*		8		9
Butter,			16		18
Beeswax,			33		
Beef,	*Bbl*	7			
Brandy 4th proof,	*Gal*	2		2	25
Corn,	*Bush*		50		
[Tear in film]					
Coffee,			34		35
Flour,	*Bbt*	6			
Flaxseed,	*Gask*	5	50	6	
Gin, American	*Gal*		75		
Lumber, pine					
Boards 1 1-4 inch	th. Ft		8		9
Scantling,			5		6
Timber, sq'r pine	40 ft	1	50	2	

---

[14] **Philip Barton Key** (1757-1815) was a Representative from the third district of Maryland. Born in Charleston, Maryland, Key pursued an academic course and later served in the British Army during the American Revolutionary War. He was taken prisoner in Florida, then sent to England and eventually released on parole. He returned to Maryland in 1785. On his return, Key studied law and was admitted to the bar in 1787. Between the fourth of March 1807 and the third of March 1813, he was elected as a Federalist to the Tenth, Eleventh and Twelfth U.S. Congresses. Key died in Georgetown, D.C., in 1815, and was interred on his estate. Later, he was reburied at Oak Hill Cemetery in Washington, D.C. Source: *Biographical Directory of the United States Congress.*

Shingles, Cypress	thou	75	
Staves, w o Hhds		15	18
k o ditto		7	7 50
w o bbls.		7	
Heading w o hhd		20	22
Lard,	Lb	10	
Molasses,	Gal	50	60
Naval Stores,			
Tar 32 Gallons,	Bbl	1 12	1 25
Rosin,		2 50	
Turpentine,			
320 lbs gross,		2	2 23
Spir. Turpentine,	Gal	37	40
Pork,	Bbl	8	9
Peas,	Bush	50	
Rum Jamaica} 4th proof,	Gal	1 50	
3d proof,		1 25	
American ditto,		70	
Rice,	100 b	1 50	1 75
Salt,	Bush	1	
Liverpool		1	
Sugar Muscovado,	100 b	12	14
Loaf,	Ll	21	22
Tobacco,	100 lb	5 50	

The True Republican or American Whig [Vol. 1. No. 3] Wilmington, NC, Tuesday, 17 January 1809, page 3, column 4. *The True Republican or American Whig* [Vol. 1. No. 8] Wilmington, NC, Tuesday, 21 February 1809, page 3, column 4. See price changes in *The True Republican or American Whig* [Vol. 1. No. 10] Wilmington, NC, Tuesday, 7 March 1809, page 3, column 1.

047. ANECDOTES. A Mr. **Dickinson**, Provost of Dundee, in Scotland, died some years since, and by will left a guinea for a poet to write an epitaph: but the executors, with an intention to defraud the poet, agreed to meet and share the guinea among them, each contributing a line to the epitaph as follows: Execu. Here lies Dickson, Provost of Dundee, 2d. Here Lies Dickson – here lies he. The third was embarrassed for some time; but at length determined to come in for his share of the guinea, vociferously bawled, Hallelujah, Hallelugee! *The True Republican or American Whig* [Vol. 1. No. 3] Wilmington, NC, Tuesday, 17 January 1809, page 4, column 1.

048. DIVISION ORDERS. HAVING appointed **Jacob Leonard** and **John F. Burgwin**, Esquires, my AIDS DE' CAMPS, they are entitled to the rank of Major, and all orders coming through either of them as such, are to be respected and obeyed accordingly. **BENJAMIN SMITH**, M. Gen., N. C. M. *The True Republican or American Whig* [Vol. 1. No. 3] Wilmington, NC, Tuesday, 17 January 1809, page 4, column 1. *The True Republican or American Whig* [Vol. 1. No. 4] Wilmington, NC, Tuesday, 24 January 1809, page 4, column 2.

049. Officers commanding the 2d, 3d and 12th brigades are requested to take the most speedy and effectual measures to detach, organize, and render to the Major General of the 6th division, Inspection Returns and Muster Rolls of the following troops, from their respective regiments, viz. Art'ry. Cav'ry. Inf'ry.} Officers included.
From 2d Brig.   85   7   432
     3d do.   60   4   315
     12th do.   63   5   334
                210   16 1080

All to be completely equipped with arms and accoutrements fit for service, including Blankets and Knapsacks. The General Officers in making a requisition of men from their several regiments will particularly designate the number and grade of Company Officers, that it will be proper to select and recommend... All proper measure should be adopted to encourage a disposition so important to the public welfare and to essential to the honor of the 6th Division of the Militia of North Carolina. By order of Major General **Smith**. JACOB LEONARD, A.D.C. Belvidere, Jan. 7, 1809. *The True Republican or American Whig* [Vol. 1. No. 3] Wilmington, NC, Tuesday, 17 January 1809, page 4, columns 1 & 2. *The True Republican or American Whig* [Vol. 1. No. 4] Wilmington, NC, Tuesday, 24 January 1809, page 4, columns 2 & 3.

050. CONGRESS. HOUSE OF REPRESENTATIVES. Wednesday, January 4. DISTRESSED SEAMEN. Mr. **Newton** offered a resolution directing the Committee of Commerce and Manufactures to enquire the propriety of providing for the relief of distressed and disabled seamen... NAVAL ESTABLISHEMENT. Mr. **Story** said, that if the House did not wish to be considered as slumbering at their posts, it was proper that they should after determining that they would not submit to the orders and decrees of the belligerents, adopt some efficient system of warfare, if war must be the result... EMBARGO. Mr. **Van Cortlandt** observed that it was impossible for the House to get along with business till the question of repeal or continuance of the embargo was decided... Thursday, January 5. ENFORCING THE EMBARGO. On motion of Mr. **Nicholas**, the House resolved itself into a committee of the whole, Mr. **Basset** in the chair on the bill for enforcing the embargo, and the several acts supplementary thereto... Saturday, December 7. EXTRA SESSION OF CONGRESS. The House were engaged till near five o'clock today in discussing the following resolution . . . whether it would not be proper, before the first day of December, viz., in the middle of May or beginning of June, essentially to change the attitude of the nation, if no change took place in the measures of foreign powers? . . Most of those who supported it declared it as their opinion that unless foreign powers revoked their orders and decrees at an early day, it would be proper to raise the embargo and substitute war and that it behooved Congress to be at their posts to take this important step. *The True Republican or American Whig* [Vol. 1. No. 4] Wilmington, NC, Tuesday, 24 January 1809, page 2, columns 2 & 3.

051. THE TRUE REPUBLICAN. WILMINGTON, Tuesday, January 24, 1809. The insults this country has sustained from England, during the last few years, are too palpable for denial and too atrocious for excuse. Yet, although a single injury has not been atoned for, or even any serious offer of atonement made, it is no uncommon thing to see, in American newspapers a marked preference given to every thing politically English. England is the scale and the model by which to regulate almost every ramification of our national institutions and national principles. We are very far from ascribing such opinions to the Editor of the *Wilmington Gazette*. It would appear, however that he had caught some little portion of the Anglo-mania, we have alluded to... But even on the ground which the Editor of the *Gazette* has assumed, we might venture to say he can be refuted... The remainders of the Editor's remarks are confined to our declaration "that it should be our task to lessen and destroy the opposition." On this occasion he has not treated us with his usual candor... But the patriotic Editor need not be alarmed. So long as the Republican Party continues in office, he may be assured that there will be an opposition composed of thousands and tens of thousands. Were an Angel from Heaven to descend and advocate the purity and wisdom of the present administration – the Editor need not fear – there would be many to think him an impertinent intruder who knew nothing of the matter, and who could have traveled such a distance only for some insidious purpose. *The True Republican or American Whig* [Vol. 1. No. 4] Wilmington, NC, Tuesday, 24 January 1809, page 3, columns 1 & 2.

052. A complete return of the late election for a President and Vice President of the United States has been received at the seat of government – We congratulate the nation on the glorious result. The votes are For President,

JAMES MADISON,	122
C. C. Pinckney,	42
George Clinton,	6

Vice President,

GEORGE CLINTON,	116
Rufus King,	48
John Langdon,	9
James Madison,	3
James Monroe,	3

The True Republican or American Whig [Vol. 1. No. 4] Wilmington, NC, Tuesday, 24 January 1809, page 3, column 2.

053. FROM THE (Boston) *DETECTOR*. Important and Interesting! – Capt. **Hall**, of the Sch. Jane, (belonging to **J. C. Jones**, Esq.) arrived here last evening from Oporto, which place he left on the 25th Nov. He states, that before he sailed, news was received there, and published, of a general engagement having taken place between the main armies of France & Spain, in which the Spaniards are said to have been defeated with the loss of thirty thousand men! . . . *The True Republican or American Whig* [Vol. 1. No. 4] Wilmington, NC, Tuesday, 24 January 1809, page 3, column 2.

054. A letter from St. Lucar, to a gentleman in New York, says, "There are now several cargoes of fish on hand at Cadiz . . . our ports are overwhelming with colonial goods and British fabrics, upon which the adventurous must meet heavy losses."

Prices Current at Surinam, Oct. 9; flour 60 dollars per barrel; beef 50; pork 65; tar 40. This place, like many of the islands, is under British protection, and probably must have large supplies of provision from the ample commercial field in which her protector proves undisturbed. Britain keeping the seas to herself is like a man's keeping tavern without any provisions for his guests.

He's gone, he's gone! Strong hints are given in some of the Southern papers, that Mr. **John Randolph** has at last fallen into a state of political insanity, and voted with the minority, against Campbell's Resolutions, *intoto*, the last resort for American honor. . . *The True Republican or American Whig* [Vol. 1. No. 4] Wilmington, NC, Tuesday, 24 January 1809, page 3, column 2.

055. Shocking to Humanity. A duel was fought on Monday the 5th inst. Between Lieut. **Wm. Littlejohn** of the army of the U.S. and Dr. **Peyton**, both natives of Louden County, in Virginia, without Seconds. The circumstances which gave rise to this unhappy affair are of a nature too delicate for publication. The moment Lieut. **Littlejohn** received the information which gave rise to the misunderstanding, he prepared his pistols and rode in pursuit of the Doctor, (who was that morning gone to the country, on a visit to one of his patients) met him in the road within one mile of Leesburg, and immediately demanded satisfaction, the Dr. replied, that he would give him the satisfaction demanded, but requested permission to go to see his family first, which request was refused by the Lieut., who declared most positively that if the Doctor did not immediately accept one of the pistols, he would blow him through. The Doctor then accepted one of the pistols; they took their stand at about 24 feet distance. The Doctor's pistol went off first and missed the Lieut. who then deliberately walked up to the Doctor, and shot him through the breast, the Dr. expired in a few minutes. We are informed a jury was called, who brought in a verdict of WILLFUL MURDER. – *Staunton Eagle*. *The True Republican or American Whig* [Vol. 1. No. 4] Wilmington, NC, Tuesday, 24 January 1809, page 3, column 3.

056. Mentor is informed that want of room alone prevents us from publishing his communications in today's paper. We shall give him a hearing next week – In the mean time, we would solicit a continuance of his correspondence. *The True Republican or American Whig* [Vol. 1. No. 4] Wilmington, NC, Tuesday, 24 January 1809, page 3, column 3.

057. COLLECTOR'S OFFICE, Port of Wilmington, N.C. January 23d, 1809. NOTICE IS HEREBY GIVEN, THAT the Act to enforce and make more effectual an Act entitled "An Act laying an Embargo on all ships and vessels in the ports and harbors of the United States," and the several Acts supplementary thereto, was passed on the 9th Inst., and received at this Office this day. . . N.B. The above section relates to all vessels, other than those whose employment has been uniformly confined to the navigation of Bays, Sounds, Rivers and Lakes within the jurisdiction of the United States. **ROBERT COCHRAN**, COLLECTOR. *The True Republican or American Whig* [Vol. 1. No. 4] Wilmington, NC, Tuesday, 24 January 1809, page 3, column 4.

058. AT A MEETING of the COMMISSIONERS OF THE Town, on Saturday, January 21, 1809. ORDERED That no Straw, Fodder, or Hay of any kind, be kept in any Kitchen, Cellar, or out Houses, except in Stables; under the penalty of forty shillings for each and every offence, after the 28th instant. By order of the Commissioners, **THOS. CALLENDER**, T. Clerk. January 24. *The True Republican or American Whig* [Vol. 1. No. 4] Wilmington, NC, Tuesday, 24 January 1809, page 3, column 4. *The True Republican or American Whig* [Vol. 1. No. 7] Wilmington, NC, Tuesday, 14 February 1809, page 4, column 3. *The True Republican or American Whig* [Vol. 1. No. 8] Wilmington, NC, Tuesday, 21 February 1809, page 4, column 4.

059. From the *Washington Monitor*. MR. **PICKERING** CONFUTED. The speech of Mr. **Pickering** on the proposed resolution of Mr. **Hillhouse** to repeal the laws laying an embargo is before the public in a pamphlet and likewise in the newspaper it will appear in the *Monitor* in regular order. In the meantime, however, the new doctrine which that gentle man has broached is doing mischief, because the impressions which it is calculated to make are not justified by facts. . *The True Republican or American Whig* [Vol. 1. No. 4] Wilmington, NC, Tuesday, 24 January 1809, page 4, column 1.

060. DOCUMENTS Accompanying the following Message from the President. To the Senate and House of Representatives of the United States. I communicate to Congress certain letters which passed between the British Secretary of State, Mr. **Canning**, and Mr. **Pinckney**, our minister plenipotentiary at London. . . The letter of Mr. **Canning**, however, having lately appeared in print, unaccompanied by that of Mr. **Pinckney** in reply, and having a tendency to make impressions not warranted by the statements of Mr. **Pinckney**, it has become proper that the whole should be brought into public view. **TH: JEFFERSON**. January 17, 1809.

Mr. **Pinckney** to Mr. **Madison**. LONDON, September 24, 1808. SIR, I am now enabled to transmit to you only last night to my note of the 23^d of August. This answer was accompanied by a letter, of which also a copy is enclosed, recapitulating what Mr. **Canning** supposes to be "the substance of what has passed between us at our several interviews previous to the presentation of my official letter." Your most obedient humble servant, **WM. PINCKNEY**. *The True Republican or American Whig* [Vol. 1. No. 7] Wilmington, NC, Tuesday, 14 February 1809, page 1, column 1.

061. [Here follows Mr. **Canning**'s letter which was published in our last.] Mr. **Pinckney** to Mr. **Canning**. GREAT CUMBERLAND PLACE, September 24, 1808. SIR, I have the honor to acknowledge the receipt of your answer to my official note of the 23d of last month, relative to the British orders in council of January and November 1807; together with a statement of "the substance of what has passed between us at our several interviews previous to the presentation of that note." I shall lose no time in transmitting to my government copies of both these papers, upon the last of which I will take the liberty in the course of a few days, to trouble you with some observations. I have the honor to be, With the highest consideration, Sir, Your most obedient humble servant, (Signed) **WILLIAM PINCKNEY**. The right honorable **George Canning**, Etc. *The True Republican or American Whig* [Vol. 1. No. 7] Wilmington, NC, Tuesday, 14 February 1809, page 1, column 2.

062. Mr. **Pinckney** to Mr. **Madison**. LONDON, October 11, 1808. SIR, I have the honor to transmit enclosed, a copy of my reply to Mr. **Canning**'s letter to me of the 23d of last month, accompanying his official answer of the same date to my note of the 23d of August. I have the honor to be, With the highest consideration, Sir, Your most obedient humble servant, (Signed) **WILLIAM PINCKNEY**. The honorable **James Madison**, Etc. Etc. Etc. *The True Republican or American Whig* [Vol. 1. No. 7] Wilmington, NC, Tuesday, 14 February 1809, page 1, column 2.

063. GREAT CUMBERLAND PLACE, October 10, 1808. SIR, If my reply to the letter, which you did me the honor to address to me on the 23d of last month, should be of greater length than the occasion may be thought to require you will I am sure impute it to its real cause, an earnest desire on my part arising from a footing of sincere respect for you, that the statement, which I am to give of facts deemed by you to be important shall be full as well as accurate. . . I say, "without any adequate necessity according to your own showing;" for I am persuaded sir, you do not mean to tell us, as upon a hasty perusal of your answer to my note might be imagined, that those rights and interests are to be set at naught, lest "a doubt should remain to distant times of the determination and the ability of Great Britain to have continued her resistance," or that your orders may, indefinitely, give a new law to the ocean, left the motive to their repeal should be mistaken by your enemy. If this might indeed, be so, you will perhaps permit me to say that, highly as we may be disposed to prize the firm attitude and vast means of your country at this moment, it would possibly suggest to some minds a reluctant doubt on the subject of your observation, "that the strength and power of Great Britain are not for herself only, but for the world." (Mr. **Pinckney**'s letter concluded in our next) *The True Republican or American Whig* [Vol. 1. No. 7] Wilmington, NC, Tuesday, 14 February 1809, page 1, columns 2 -4 and page 2, columns 1-3. MR. **PINCKNEY**'S LETTER TO MR. **CANNING**. (Concluded.) I might also have been led to intimate that my proposal could apparently lose nothing by admitting that "by some unfortunate concurrence of circumstances, without any hostile intention, the American embargo did come in aid of the" before mentioned "blockade of European continent, precisely at the very moment when, if that blockade could have succeeded at all, this interposition of the American government would most effectually have contributed to its success." . . . **WILLIAM PINCKNEY**. *The True Republican or American Whig* [Vol. 1. No. 8] Wilmington, NC, Tuesday, 21 February 1809, page 1, columns 1 – 4.

064. LATE FOREIGN INTELLIGENCE. On the 24th ult. Arrived at New York the British Packer Princess Amelia Morson, from Falmouth, via Bermuda, having left England on the 8th of December: and the ship Philipsburgh of Lessingwell, from Liverpool and Cork. The latter left Liverpool on the 7th of November and Cork on the 12 December. By these vessels London papers to the 3d and Cork papers to the 8th of December have been received. Mr. **Purviance**, passenger in the Philipsburgh, is the bearer of Dispatches to our government. Two British regiments of cavalry sailed from Falmouth from Spain on the 6th of December. On the 24th of Nov. the Lavinia sailed from England with the Spanish deputies, and 1,500,000 dollars on board. The accounts of military operations in Spain are confuted. Of those, however, received, the following is a comprehensive sketch. . . *The True Republican or American Whig* [Vol. 1. No. 7] Wilmington, NC, Tuesday, 14 February 1809, page 2, columns 3 & 4.

065. IMPEACHMENT. In the House of Representatives, on the 25th ult. Mr. **Quincy**, ('the Burke and Windham of America, united,' as Mr. [William] **Hasell** says) after some prefatory observations, submitted five distinct charges against the President of the United States, wherein he accuses him of forcing the late Collector of Boston, a Federalist, to continue in office! After considerable debate, the quest on was taken on considering the resolution, and negative, - Yea, Mr. **Quincy** – 1. Nays 117. . . *The True Republican or American Whig* [Vol. 1. No. 7] Wilmington, NC, Tuesday, 14 February 1809, page 2, column 4 and page 3, columns 1 & 2.

066. NOTICE. ON Wednesday, the first of March next, will be exposed to sale at Public Auction in Wilmington, for gold or silver coin, the Schooner called the THEODA, of about 80 tons burthen, with her furniture, & c. – Also, a quantity of Shingles, Staves, and Heading condemned

for the benefit of the United States, and ordered to be sold by a decree of the district court for the district of Cape Fear. **J. C. DUNBIBIN**, D. Marshal Feb. 14. *The True Republican or American Whig* [Vol. 1. No. 7] Wilmington, NC, Tuesday, 14 February 1809, page 3, column 2. *The True Republican or American Whig* [Vol. 1. No. 8] Wilmington, NC, Tuesday, 21 February 1809, page 4, column 3.

067. NOTICE. ON Wednesday, the first of March next, will be exposed to sale at Public Auction in Wilmington, for gold or silver coin, the Lugger[15] called the FAIR TRADER, of about one hundred & fifteen tons burthen, with her furniture, & condemned for the benefit of the United States and ordered to be sold by a decree of the district court for the district of Cape Fear. **J. C. DUNBIBIN**, D. Marshal Feb. 14. *The True Republican or American Whig* [Vol. 1. No. 7] Wilmington, NC, Tuesday, 14 February 1809, page 3, column 2. *The True Republican or American Whig* [Vol. 1. No. 8] Wilmington, NC, Tuesday, 21 February 1809, page 4, column 3.

068. NOTICE. THE Subscriber has purchased from Dr. **Everitt**,[16] the Schooner Telegraph, and intends to run her as a packet, between Smithville and Wilmington, and solicits employment. **THOMAS SMITH**. Feb. 12. 2w. *The True Republican or American Whig* [Vol. 1. No. 7] Wilmington, NC, Tuesday, 14 February 1809, page 3, column 2. *The True Republican or American Whig* [Vol. 1. No. 8] Wilmington, NC, Tuesday, 21 February 1809, page 4, column 3.

069. Valuable land for Sale. THE Subscriber offers for sale that valuable Plantation, formerly owned by **James Clark**, lying on Goshen, in Duplin County. It contains about 328 acres; a considerable part of which is cleared and under good fences. An excellent Dwelling House, out houses, and other necessary improvements, is on the premises: and the situation is at least equal to any in the county. The terms of sale will be made known on application to Mr. **Samuel Dunn**, near the premises. **WM. DUNN**. Newbern, Feb. 10. *The True Republican or American Whig* [Vol. 1. No. 7] Wilmington, NC, Tuesday, 14 February 1809, page 3, column 2. *The True Republican or American Whig* [Vol. 1. No. 9] Wilmington, NC, Tuesday, 28 February 1809, page 1, column 4. *The True Republican or American Whig* [Vol. 1. No. 10] Wilmington, NC, Tuesday, 7 March 1809, page 3, column 1.

070. The True Republican. WILMINGTON, Tuesday, February 14, 1809. The following letter, written by a gentleman in Marblehead, to a merchant in this town, under date of the 21st of last month, breathes such a pure spirit of patriotism, and so correctly displays the politics and shameful intrigues of the Effex Junta, that we feel gratified in the permission to present it to our readers. "The non-intercourse bill, together with the determination to enforce the embargo, have, (as you conjecture,) made great changes in our market for all foreign goods - . . . A war with England is considered inevitable. What alteration it will make in our market, is uncertain; but at present there is no prospect of obtaining more for tobacco and cotton than the prices quoted by you. . . *The True Republican or American Whig* [Vol. 1. No. 7] Wilmington, NC, Tuesday, 14 February 1809, page 3, columns 3 & 4.

---

[15] A **lugger** is a small fishing or coasting boat that carries one or more lugsails and that has two or three masts with or without jibs or topsails. A lugsail is a four-sided sail bent to a yard that hangs more or less obliquely on a mast slung at about a third or quarter of it length from the forward end and hoisted and lowered with the sail, called also a lug.

[16] **Reuben Everitt** (1761-1811) was a physician and surgeon to the troops at Fort Johnston, Smithville, North Carolina. In July 1801 he offered his medicine and professional services in Wilmington, at the corner store south side of Market - wharf. He died 1 February 1811 at the age of 50 and his remains were buried in the Smithville town cemetery. *Wilmington Gazette*, Wilmington, NC, Thursday, 6 August 1801, [Vol. 5, No. 239] page 3, editor **Allmand Hall**. Thanks to the William Reaves Collection, New Hanover Public Library and also Ida B. Kellam, *Lower Cape Fear Gravestone Records Vol. 1* (1959).

071. The Secretary of State for foreign affairs of his Royal Highness, the Prince Regent of Portugal[17] has officially informed Mr. [**Henry**] **Hill**, the American consul, at St. Salvador, that vessels of the U. S. will be treated in the port of Brazil as those of the most favored nation. *The True Republican or American Whig* [Vol. 1. No. 7] Wilmington, NC, Tuesday, 14 February 1809, page 3, column 4.

072. Communicated – It is hinted, that since Mr. **Quincy** has failed in his attempt to impeach the President for not turning out a Federalist from office, he is determined to have a slap at him on account of his red breeches. If he fails in this, the heinous crime committed by the President, of fastening his horse to a peg, will be the next "high crime and misdemeanor" which will come in for a share of this gentleman's wrath. *Petersburg Rep. The True Republican or American Whig* [Vol. 1. No. 7] Wilmington, NC, Tuesday, 14 February 1809, page 3, column 4.

073. Port of Wilmington. ENTERED. Brig Reliance, **Darrell**, New York. Brig Virginia, **Richardson**, Charleston [SC]. Sch'r Patty, **Baker**, New York. Sch'r Harmony, **Hopkins**, Rio Janeiro. Sloop Patty, **McLean**, Charleston [SC]. CLEARED. Sch'r Return, **Garrot**, Charleston [SC]. Sch'r Venus, **Oliver**, New York. Sch'r Ann Eliza, **Ruggles**, Providence. Sloop George, **Dennison**, Salem, Mass. Sch'r Anne, **Dunham**, Boston. Sch'r Regulator, **McIlhenny**, Charleston [SC]. Sch'r Amanda, **Davidson**, New York. *The True Republican or American Whig* [Vol. 1. No. 7] Wilmington, NC, Tuesday, 14 February 1809, page 3, column 4.

074. FOR THE TRUE REPUBLICAN. The best privileges are often abused. The freedom of the press is one characteristic of a republic, the right of speech another: both are frequently abused, the latter, however, be it ever so much perverted and the greatest latitude allowed it, will but seldom do any material injury: the former, notwithstanding it is as in correct a source as the other, . . MENTOR. *The True Republican or American Whig* [Vol. 1. No. 7] Wilmington, NC, Tuesday, 14 February 1809, page 4, columns 1 & 2.

075. PATRIOT. The Legislature of Massachusetts met on the 25th ult. When Lieut. Governor [**Levi**] **Lincoln** addressed that body in a speech replete with genuine patriotism. . . *The True Republican or American Whig* [Vol. 1. No. 8] Wilmington, NC, Tuesday, 21 February 1809, page 2, columns & 2.

076. From the *Aurora*. PHILADELPHIA CITY AND COUNTY MEETING. Yesterday being appointed by a call upon the friends of the union, independence and commerce, for meeting at the Statehouse, . a number of persons composed of men hostile to the peace and the principles of the

---

[17] **John VI** (1767-1826) prince regent of Portugal from 1799 to 1816, and king from 1816 to 1826, whose reign saw the revolutionary struggle in France, the Napoleonic invasion of Portugal (during which he established his court in Brazil, and the implantation of representative government in both Portugal and Brazil.) John was the younger son of **Queen Maria I** (1734-1816), becoming heir on her death. On the seventeenth of November 1807, an army of French and Spanish soldiers under the command of the French General **Andoche Junot** entered Portugal and marched on Lisbon. The British were in no position to defend their ally; consequently, the prince regent and the royal family left for Brazil. On 27 November, Junot's army took control of Lisbon. The *Wilmington Gazette* printed on 15 December 1807, "In coming through the Downs [Area of sea in the English Channel], Capt. **M'Lachlan** was boarded by several British cruisers, and treated with politeness. October 30, in lat. 35 15, long. 19, was boarded by the British lugger Alarm, Capt. **Wilkins**, who informed, that a few days before, he had fallen in with the Portuguese fleet, from Lisbon for the Brazils, having on board the Queen, Prince Regent, and most of the Nobility attached to the Court of Portugal. Lisbon had been taken possession of by the French troop's whey they sailed. The fleet consisted of 33 sail, 17 of which were ships of the line, convoyed by the British." *The Wilmington Gazette* [Number 571. 11th Year] Wilmington, NC, Tuesday, 15 December 1807, page 2, column 4.

government, some few lawyers, **Robert Wharton**, the late mayor of this city, and persons of this cast entered the State House Yard, . . . A body of sailors was called upon the preceding evening, and Commodore **Truxton** was selected to be made the instrument of this unworthy proceeding. . . A few minutes before 11 o'clock, Capt. **William Jones** was called to the chair, and Col. **Robert M'Mullin** appointed Secretary by the unanimous voice of the EIGHTEEN THOUSAND Citizens who were there assembled. . . After a number of patriotic resolutions were passed, General **Barker**, the mayor of this city delivered a very popular and pointed speech . . . we understand he narrated the conduct of **Timothy Pickering**, in the café of several American citizens, who were detained and pressed on board a British sloop of war, at Philadelphia wharf, when **Pickering** was Secretary of State. . . After several speakers had closed Mr. **J. Leib** moved, that as a gross misrepresentation, that the citizens present, march in procession down Chestnut Street through Second into Dock, (by the British Coffee House,) and there disperse. *The True Republican or American Whig* [Vol. 1. No. 8] Wilmington, NC, Tuesday, 21 February 1809, page 2, columns 2 & 3.

077. The nomination of General **Dearborn**, as Collector of the port of Boston, has been approved by the Senate – Yeas 25, -- Nays 7. *The True Republican or American Whig* [Vol. 1. No. 8] Wilmington, NC, Tuesday, 21 February 1809, page 3, column 4.

078. "MENTOR" was handed in too late for today's paper. His *Communication* shall appear in our next. *The True Republican or American Whig* [Vol. 1. No. 8] Wilmington, NC, Tuesday, 21 February 1809, page 3, column 4.

079. Married, ON Tuesday evening, by the Rev. **Solomon Halling**,[18] Mr. **Hugh Campbell**, Merchant of Fayetteville, to Miss **Henrietta Ann Mallett**, daughter of the late **Peter Mallett**, *Esq. The True Republican or American Whig* [Vol. 1. No. 8] Wilmington, NC, Tuesday, 21 February 1809, page 3, column 4.

080. NOTICE. THE SUBSCRIBER INFORMS the Inhabitants of Wilmington and its Vicinity, that he has taken the new Brick-House in Second Street, a little north of the market and opposite Mr. **Gilbert Geers**, where he has opened a HOTEL. ALL those, who will favor him with their company, shall be accommodated with the best that the Wilmington markets afford, and due respect paid to his Customers. **JOHN HOUSTON**. February 10. 3w. *The True Republican or American Whig* [Vol. 1. No. 8] Wilmington, NC, Tuesday, 21 February 1809, page 3, column 4. *The True Republican or American Whig* [Vol. 1. No. 9] Wilmington, NC, Tuesday, 28 February 1809, page 1, column 4. *The True Republican or American Whig* [Vol. 1. No. 10] Wilmington, NC, Tuesday, 7 March 1809, page 4, column 4.

081. ANECDOTE. Two Lawyers, one day, in riding the road, came up with a Clergyman. Says one of them to his fellow traveler, "We'll crack a joke upon the priest." Pleased with the idea of their sport, they rode up, one on either side. After mutual salutations, one of them says, "How happens it, daddy, that gentlemen of your cloth make such egregious blunders in the pulpit? I heard one not long since, when he wished to say, Og, King of Basham, say "Hog, king of Bacon." "Oh," replied the divine, "We are men of like infirmities with the rest of our fellow creatures; I lately, when I should have said, the devil is the father of liars – said, the devil is the father of lawyers?" "Ah," replied the other, "Which are you, a knave or a fool?" "I believe, gentlemen," he

---

[18] The Rev. Dr. **Solomon Halling** (1754-1813) served as pastor of Saint James Church in Wilmington, North Carolina from 1795 to 1809. He was a surgeon in the Continental Line 4th NC in 1779 until the end of the American Revolutionary War of Independence in 1783. The earliest records of Saint James Parish have been destroyed or lost. There are no known registers from the establishment of the parish in 1729 to 1811. On 17 February 1809, **Solomon Halling** gave to his granddaughter **Ann Eliza Usher** a Negro female child named **Eliza**. The deed was witnessed by **Thomas Watson** & **John Ramsey**. New Hanover County Deed Book O, page 58. Thank you to Dr. A. B. Pruitt, *Abstracts of Deeds New Hanover Co, NC Books N & O* (2006).

replied, "I am BETWEEN BOTH." *The True Republican or American Whig* [Vol. 1. No. 8] Wilmington, NC, Tuesday, 21 February 1809, page 4, column 2.

082. To the Public. FOR some time past, I have heard of a charge brought against me in the *Wilmington Gazette*, by a certain **Moses Manning**, the writer of which is **John Felix Rhodes**: Which charge, I acknowledge in part, and will point out my reasons for so doing. It is with the sincerest reluctance I have recourse to this method of declaring myself, and for various causes; -- *First,* I am painfully convinced, it will injure the feelings that worthy family, to wit: -- the **Houston**'s, into which he married. *Secondly,* -- on account of his wife, . . . who is now reduced to suffering through his shameful conduct, -- *Thirdly,* -- on account of his Brothers and Sisters, . . . He (the said **Rhodes**) had previously and repeatedly been charged of being guilty of *Forgery*, such as drawing note for sums of money and signing other mens' names thereto, without even their knowledge or content. . . On my making the request **Rhodes** immediately replied, "By G—d I can uncle Billy, [19] and that comp leady and will, if you say so," which I confess, astonished me, and of course confirmed in my opinion what he had been previously charged with. . . be sufficient to constitute him as such, I pronounce **John Felix Rhodes**, a *thief* and a *liar*. As for a certain **Moses Manning**, who has been endeavoring to propagate a number of absurd lies against me, I should leave him here entirely unnoticed, were the public acquainted with his character. . . **WM. SOUTHERLAND**. DUPLIN, January 28, 1809. 3t. *The True Republican or American Whig* [Vol. 1. No. 8] Wilmington, NC, Tuesday, 21 February 1809, page 4, columns 2 & 3. *The True Republican or American Whig* [Vol. 1. No. 9] Wilmington, NC, Tuesday, 28 February 1809, page 4, columns 2 & 3. *The True Republican or American Whig* [Vol. 1. No. 10] Wilmington, NC, Tuesday, 7 March 1809, page 4, columns 2 & 3.

083. CELEBRTION of the FOURTH MARCH, 1809. Such Citizens of Wilmington and its Vicinity as may be disposed to celebrate the triumph of correct principles, in the Election of **James Madison** to the Presidency of the United States, are informed that a Subscription paper for that purpose is deposited at Mr. **OWEN KENAN**'S Store. Feb. 28. *The True Republican or American Whig* [Vol. 1. No. 9] Wilmington, NC, Tuesday, 28 February 1809, page 3, column 2.

084. The Subscriber UNDER the present circumstances, is compelled to decline selling any longer on credit, he requests all persons indebted to him by note or open accounts, to call and settle the same; those who will neglect to do it, must expect that their notes or accounts, will be placed in the hands of an attorney, to be sued for at the next County Court, which will occasion expenses which the Subscriber is anxious to avoid. **JOHN GARNIER**. February 21. 2w. *The True Republican or American Whig* [Vol. 1. No. 9] Wilmington, NC, Tuesday, 28 February 1809, page 3, column 2. *The True Republican or American Whig* [Vol. 1. No. 10] Wilmington, NC, Tuesday, 7 March 1809, page 4, column 4.

085. Five Dollars Reward. Ran away From The Subscriber, ABOUT three weeks ago, a Negro Man, named **JACK**; well known in and about Wilmington – Any person that will deliver the above Negro to me in Brunswick County or to **Owen Kenan**, in Wilmington, shall receive the above reward. **THOMAS SMITH**. February 28. 2w. *The True Republican or American Whig* [Vol. 1. No. 9.] 28 February 1809, page 3, column 2. *The True Republican or American Whig* [Vol. 1. No. 11] Wilmington, NC, Tuesday, 14 March 1809, page 2, column 4.

086. STOP THE SWINDLERS! 1000 Dollars reward. Will be paid for the apprehending and delivery of **JOHN THOMAS** and **HONORE MONPOEY**, who absconded from this city on

---

[19] To slander someone *Uncle Billy* is to call a man similar to the portrayal of the main African-American character in Harriet Beecher Stowe's antislavery novel *Uncle Tom's Cabin* (1852). ***Comp leady*** or *compound larceny*, is the offense committed by a person who, having been directly injured by a felony, agrees with the criminal that he will not prosecute him, on condition of the latter's making reparation, or on receipt of a reward or bribe not to prosecute. Henry C. Black, *Black's Law Dictionary* (St. Paul, MN: West Pub. Co. 1983) page 150.

Tuesday or Wednesday last having swindled several persons to a considerable amount. **JOHN THOMAS** is a small thick set well made man, about 5 feet 4 inches high, 34 or 35 years of age, dark complexion, short black hair, and a very black beard; speaks fast, and usually with a smile in his countenance; has a remarkable scar on the side of his face; much inclined to dress; pretends to have some knowledge of horses, and frequently rides on a good one. Said **THOMAS** resided for many years in Union Street, where he kept a boarding house and grocery store.

HONORE MONPOEY is about 5 feet 9 or 10 inches high, a Creole of St. Domingo, speaks broken English, of slender make, is lame in one foot, has a dark swarthy complexion, with short coarse curly hair, so much so that many would not take him for a white man, but from his residence in this city for many years past, he has generally been considered as such, pitted with the small pox, speaks fast tho' he stammers while he speaks usually very slovenly in his dress, pretend to have a knowledge of horses, having latterly been in the habit of trafficking in the above species of property, as well as letting public hairs. **MONPOEY** resided at the corner of Wentworth and King Streets, where he kept a grocery store. From their connections, it is highly probable they have traveled the same road, and may make for St. Mary's, Georgia or New Orleans. FIVE HINDRED DOLLARS reward will be paid for apprehending and delivering either; or ONE THOUSAND DOLLARS for both. **Washington Potter**, **William Porter**, **Daniel Latham, Philip Cohen, Joshua Brown**} Committee in behalf of the Creditors. Charleston, [SC] Feb. 20. *The True Republican or American Whig* [Vol. 1. No. 9.] Wilmington, NC, Tuesday, 28 February 1809, page 3, column 2. *The True Republican or American Whig* [Vol. 1. No. 10] Wilmington, NC, Tuesday, 7 March 1809, page 4, column 4. *The True Republican or American Whig* [Vol. 1. No. 11] Wilmington, NC, Tuesday, 14 March 1809, page 3, column 4.

087. No papers north of Raleigh have been received since our last publication. -- We are pleased to learn that our Representative in Congress has effected a very desirable alteration in the conveyance of the Duplin mail. A post office has been established at the new court house in that county, at which place, after some time in April, a mail will continue to be opened. *The True Republican or American Whig* [Vol. 1. No. 9.] Wilmington, NC, Tuesday, 28 February 1809, page 3, column 3.

088. Port of Wilmington. ENTERED. Sch'r Milly, **Rhodes**, Charleston. CLEARED. Sloop Patty, **McLean**, Charleston. Ship Abeona, **Hitch**, Philadelphia. Sch'r Rover, **Winkoy**, New-River. Sch'r Isabella, **Barkman**, Exuma. *The True Republican or American Whig* [Vol. 1. No. 9.] Wilmington, NC, Tuesday, 28 February 1809, page 3, column 4.

089. FOR THE TRUE REPUBLICAN. I have seen two pieces in the *Wilmington Gazette*, one under the signature "Leonidas," and the other "The Ghost of Telamaheus." From the similarity of diction existing between the two, I may venture to infer that the author of one is the author of the other, and that both are the offspring of the same contaminated brain – the airy visions of the same polluted imagination. My object in preparing for publicity the pieces signed "Mentor," (which has already appeared in the "True Republican") was, to expose the enemies of the American Government – the Tories and disorganizers of the day – to apprize the public of their domestic foes and be well applied accusations to discover whether Wilmington was infested with such filthy characters. Not wishing in the commencement of my "grand attack" to take the poor devils by surprise, I resolved in perfect good humour, to talk with and convince them of what they might in case of combat, expect from "Mentor." Having thus warned the creatures, I purposed to twitch'em las & belabour their carcasses, til the whole clan should bawl out enough. . . In the mean time, farewell until next week, when you may look out for a continuation of the subject. MENTOR. *The True Republican or American Whig* [Vol. 1. No. 9.] Wilmington, NC, Tuesday, 28 February 1809, page 4, columns 1 & 2. *Continued, The True Republican or American Whig* [Vol. 1. No. 10] Wilmington, NC, Tuesday, 7 March 1809, page 4, column 1.

090. The True Republican will henceforth be conducted under the firm of **WATSON & RAMSEY**. *The True Republican or American Whig* [Vol. 1. No. 10] Wilmington, NC, Tuesday, 7 March 1809, page 3, column 2.

091. THE FOURTH OF MARCH, 1809, Being the day of Mr. **Madison**'s inauguration as President of the United States; it was celebrated in this town with demonstrations of great joy. The military paraded; and at 12 o'clock fired salutes. The Gun Boat commanded by Captain **Gautier** beautifully dressed with a variety of colours was hauled into the stream opposite Market Street. At noon it fired a salute, as did also, some other vessels in the harbour. At 3 o'clock, a very numerous company, composed of those friendly to the election of Mr. **Madison**, sat down to a dinner, prepared for the occasion by Mr. **Dick**, at the Court House. **Joshua Potts**, Esq. President. **A. F. MacNeill**, Esq. Vice President. After Dinner, the following toasts were drank; followed by appropriate Music and firing of Guns: . . . 14th., The State and Governor of North Carolina. 15th, The late Elector of this District -- the venerable patriot, **Samuel Ashe**, Sen'r. 16th, **Thos. Kenan**, Esquire, our Representative in Congress, of the U. States. 17th, The American Fair. VOLUNTEERS. *By the President* -- The rights of the citizens of the United States, in life, liberty, and property, and may free ships constitute free goods. *By the Vice-President* -- The eloquent and patriotic **William B. Giles**, Senator in the Congress of the United States. *By Captain Gautier* -- Peace before War; *By Capt. Dudley, jun.* -- Gun Boat, No. 7. *By Mr. I. Cowan* -- The town of Wilmington -- unanimity and friendship amongst its inhabitants. *By Mr. Wingate* -- Commodore **Stephen Decatur**, of Tripolitan[20] memory. *By Mr. M'Call* -- General **James Wilkinson**, Commander in Chief of the American Army. After the President had retired -- *Joshua Potts,* Esq. -- Ever true to his trust. In the dusk of the Evening, the Gun Boat being splendidly illuminated, exhibited the name of Madison in large letters handsomely executed; & under one of the arches of the Court House, was displayed an elegant transparent painting, devised by Mr. **Tarbe**, and executed in a masterly manner by the ingenious Mr. **Belanger**, representing the American Eagle, in the act of angrily tearing in pieces, and spurning from it, the *Berlin Decree, Tribute & Orders in Council.*[21] On the pedestal were inscribed the seventeen United States. During the exhibition, a Band of Music continued to perform, which, together with the calm serenity of the Evening, contributed to give the whole a most pleasing and delightful effect. *The True Republican or American Whig* [Vol. 1. No. 10] Wilmington, NC, Tuesday, 7 March 1809, page 3, columns 2 & 3.

092. "THE EMBARGO TELLS," Extracts of a letter from a respectable House in Kingston, (Jamaica,) to a merchant of this place, dated January 22, 1809. "We are truly sorry to learn, that your Non-Intercourse Bill will probably pass into a law. We are fearful, it will be the cause of serious business, both to your own country and ours. . . *The True Republican or American Whig* [Vol. 1. No. 10] Wilmington, NC, Tuesday, 7 March 1809, page 3, column 3.

---

[20] Tripolitan War: (1802-1805) War between the United States and the North African state of Tripoli, to which the United States had been paying tribute, since 1784, for shipping access. The United States refused to pay in 1801, which resulted in the United States ships being attacked. The United States marines captured the town of Derna, led by Lieut. **Stephen Decatur** (1779-1820) in 1805, to end the war.

[21] Berlin Decree, 1806: Was created in response to the Orders in Council by the British, in which the French proclaimed a blockade of the British Isles, and any ship attempting to enter or leave a British port would be seized by France. The Decree was answered with another Orders in Council, in which all ships must come to England for licenses of trade. Orders in Council: In May 1806, the British followed the Essex decision with the first of several trade regulations, known as the Orders in Council, which established a blockade of part of the continent of Europe and prohibited trade with France, unless American vessels went to British ports for licenses for trade.

093. The militia of Sampson County, on the day appointed for their appearance to furnish the requisition called for by the general government, rendered their quota by a patriotic offer of their services: - Of course, there was no draft in that county. We have heard from several other counties in that state, where the numbers required was supplied by volunteers. Such, we trust, will be the spirit of the militia who have not yet been called upon. *The True Republican or American Whig* [Vol. 1. No. 10] Wilmington, NC, Tuesday, 7 March 1809, page 3, column 4.

094. The following melancholy event took place on Tuesday last [28 February 1809]. -- A striking lesson to the thoughtless and dissipated. Col. **Thomas Alston** of Franklin County, and **Tarleton Johnson** of Granville County, were at Halifax County Court, and had a violent quarrel -- when the former threatened to shoot the latter, **Johnson** in company with another person started home and had not gone more than two miles from Halifax, when Col. **Alston** overtook them and presenting a pistol at **Johnson**, snapped it twice, without effect; **Johnson** then presented his gun at **Alston**, and shot him dead on the spot.[22] The body was conveyed to Halifax, whither **Johnson** returned and surrendered to bail. [*Raleigh Register*] *The True Republican or American Whig* [Vol. 1. No. 10] Wilmington, NC, Tuesday, 7 March 1809, page 3, column 4.

095. General **Joseph Wilkinson**, of Maryland, is appointed Governor of the Mississippi Territory, in the room of **Robert Williams**, resigned. *The True Republican or American Whig* [Vol. 1. No. 10] Wilmington, NC, Tuesday, 7 March 1809, page 3, column 4.

096. Published by **WATSON & RAMSEY**, on Second, near Market Street, At three Dollars per annum, half in advance, or three Dollars and fifty Cents, if not paid within the year. *The True Republican or American Whig* [Vol. 1. No. 10] Wilmington, NC, Tuesday, 7 March 1809, page 4, column 4. *The True Republican or American Whig* [Vol. 1. No. 11] Wilmington, NC, Tuesday, 14 March 1809, page 4, column 4. *The True Republican or American Whig* [Vol. 1. No. 12] Wilmington, NC, Tuesday, 21 March 1809, page 4, column 4. *The True Republican or American Whig* [Vol. 1. No. 16] Wilmington, NC, Tuesday, 18 April 1809, page 4, column 4. *The True Republican or American Whig* [Vol. 1. No. 18] Wilmington, NC, Tuesday, 2 May 1809, page 4, column 4. *The True Republican or American Whig* [Vol. 1. No. 19] Wilmington, NC, Tuesday, 9 May 1809, page 4, column 4. *The True Republican or American Whig* [Vol. 1. No. 20] Wilmington, NC, Tuesday, 16 May 1809, page 1, column 1. *The True Republican or American Whig* [Vol. 1. No. 21] Wilmington, NC, Tuesday, 23 May 1809, page 1, column 1. *The True Republican or American Whig* [Vol. 1. No. 23] Wilmington, NC, Tuesday, 6 June 1809, page 1, column 1. *The True Republican or American Whig* [Vol. 1. No. 25] Wilmington, NC, Tuesday, 20 June 1809, page 1, column 1. *The True Republican or American Whig* [Vol. 1. No. 27] Wilmington, NC, Tuesday, 4 July 1809, page 1, column 1.

097. *From the National Intelligence.* The following are original letters of the illustrious **Washington**, most eminently adapted to the present crisis. The sentiments are sterling; such as that upright man felt from the bottom of his soul. Were he now alive, what terrors would not his indignant frown strike into the hearts of those wretches, who, for the base purpose of disaffection, of errant Toryism, of foreign attachments, dare to invoke his name: who, with the flexible malignity of the serpent, turn and twist themselves into endless contortions to deceive and seduce the unwary; who affect and retract, retract and assert, the most profligate falsehoods, with the insensibility and impudence of a stage players. *Continued. The True Republican or American Whig* [Vol. 1. No. 11] Wilmington, NC, Tuesday, 14 March 1809, page 1, columns 1, 2, 3 & 4.

098. EXTRACTS OF LETTERS Read by Mr. **Troup**, in the House of Representatives, received from gentlemen of the first respectability in Georgia. "For six or eight months last past, there has

---

[22] Died. Near Halifax, a few days ago, Col. **Thomas H. Alston**, from a gunshot wound. *Raleigh Minerva*, Thursday, 2 March 1809, 3:3. Thanks to Lois Smathers Neal (compiler), *Abstracts of Vital Records From Raleigh, North Carolina Newspapers, 1799 - 1819, Vol. 1* (Raleigh: North Carolina Genealogical Society, 1997, republished from 1979) page 8, citation number 76.

been an extensive scene of smuggling carrying on between the United States and Florida. Upwards of twenty large cargoes of provisions, cotton and timber have sailed from Amelia Island for Britain and her possessions. There is at this moment, near twenty sail of British vessels in the waters sailing into St. Mary's River, all of them loading with timber, naval stores, cotton and provisions. Most of the vessels are strongly armed - several of them mount 20 guns. In addition to this I frequently receive correct information of armed vessels being at anchor on our coast receiving cargoes from our base unprincipled inhabitants and foreign speculators.[23] If some method cannot be fallen on to put a stop to this smuggling trade there is no use in keeping the embargo on. . ." *The True Republican or American Whig* [Vol. 1. No. 11] Wilmington, NC, Tuesday, 14 March 1809, page 1, column 4 and page 2, column 1.

099. WANTED. As Apprentices to the Printing business, TWO active Boys, of about 14 or 15 years of age -- Apply at the Office of the True Republican. March 14. *The True Republican or American Whig* [Vol. 1. No. 11] Wilmington, NC, Tuesday, 14 March 1809, page 2, column 4. *The True Republican or American Whig* [Vol. 1. No. 12] Wilmington, NC, Tuesday, 21 March 1809, page 3, column 1. *The True Republican or American Whig* [Vol. 1. No. 16] Wilmington, NC, Tuesday, 18 April 1809, page 4, column 3. *The True Republican or American Whig* [Vol. 1. No. 18] Wilmington, NC, Tuesday, 2 May 1809, page 4, column 4. *The True Republican or American Whig* [Vol. 1. No. 19] Wilmington, NC, Tuesday, 9 May 1809, page 4, column 4. *The True Republican or American Whig* [Vol. 1. No. 20] Wilmington, NC, Tuesday, 16 May 1809, page 3, column 1. *The True Republican or American Whig* [Vol. 1. No. 21] Wilmington, NC, Tuesday, 23 May 1809, page 4, column 4. *The True Republican or American Whig* [Vol. 1. No. 23] Wilmington, NC, Tuesday, 6 June 1809, page 1, column 1. *The True Republican or American Whig* [Vol. 1. No. 25] Wilmington, NC, Tuesday, 20 June 1809, page 3, column 3. *The True Republican or American Whig* [Vol. 1. No. 27] Wilmington, NC, Tuesday, 4 July 1809, page 4, column 4.

100. For The True Republican. '*To Leonidas.*' . . . You wind up your paltry production by having recourse to the favourite expedient of your party, and recite a parcel of old and hackneyed falsehoods. Their authors have been proven to be liars, many years ago. It is possible, Leonidas that I may again condescend to notice you -- if I should not, my silence will be attributable to the 'contempt I feel for your writings.' MENTOR. *The True Republican or American Whig* [Vol. 1. No. 11] Wilmington, NC, Tuesday, 14 March 1809, page 3, column 2.

101. COMMUNICATION. "Why let the stricken deer go weep, The hart ungalled play." . . . an editorial paragraph in the *Gazette*, which gave a construction to the transparency, exhibited on the 4th of March, widely different from the real effect it was intended to produce. . . If the Editor of the *Wilmington Gazette*'s regret at the manifestation of party spirit, was sincere, why did he omit publishing the whole of the toasts given on the 4th of March . . . ? . . . Was the Editor of the *Gazette*'s vision eclipsed, that he could not see five dark lanthorns on board the Gun Boat? We must suppose his organs of hearing also obtuse, otherwise, he must have heard only twelve guns fired as a federal salute; but perhaps it was prudent not to criticize on Gun Boat man oeuvres. VERITAS. *The True Republican or American Whig* [Vol. 1. No. 11] Wilmington, NC, Tuesday, 14 March 1809, page 3, column 2.

102. WILMINGTON, TUESDAY, MARCH 14, 1809. Previous to adjournment, Congress passed, and the President has ratified, the bill providing for a repeal of the embargo on the 15th instant. The non-intercourse bill, has also passed - to take effect on the 20th of May. We noticed

---

[23] In spite of policy and orders to the contrary, the trade of East Florida went more and more to the United States. There, markets were more accessible and they offered a greater variety of goods at better prices. Fernandina on Amelia Island derived its importance from a combination of factors. It was a free port on the boundary between Florida and the United States, largely unpoliced by either country. The Jefferson embargo in 1807 made it the base of a vast smuggling trade, and the prohibition by the United States of the international slave trade in 1808 made it the logical center for that activity. Carlton W. Tebeau, *A History of Florida* (University of Miami Press: 1971), page 102.

its principal features in our last. *The True Republican or American Whig* [Vol. 1. No. 11] Wilmington, NC, Tuesday, 14 March 1809, page 3, column 3.

103. Married, In Onslow County, on the 6th instant, Mr. **William Hill**, of Duplin to Miss **Ann Dudley**, daughter of Col. **Christopher Dudley**, of the former place. *The True Republican or American Whig* [Vol. 1. No. 11] Wilmington, NC, Tuesday, 14 March 1809, page 3, column 4. *The Wilmington Gazette* [Number 636. 13th Year] Wilmington, NC, Tuesday, 14 March 1809, page 3, column 4.

104. Port of Wilmington. ENTERED. Sch'r Eagle, **Bostwick**, New River. Sch'r Regulator, **McIlhenny**, Charleston. Sch'r Clarissa & Eliza, **Kennedy**, Ditto. Sch'r Rover, **Bittall**, Wiscasset. Sch'r Venus, **Oliver**, New York. Brig Clarissa, **Wadham**, New York. Ship Lightfoot, **Watson**, Liverpool. CLEARED. Brig Two Friends, **Saurie**, Turks Island. Sch'r Eagle, **Goodvine**, New-River. Sch'r Polly, **Jarvis**, Topsail Sound. Brig Alexis, **Livingston**, Trinidad. Sch'r Regulator, **McIlhenny**, Charleston. Sch'r Harmony, **Hopkins**, Boston. *The True Republican or American Whig* [Vol. 1. No. 11] Wilmington, NC, Tuesday, 14 March 1809, page 3, column 4. *The Wilmington Gazette* [Number 636. 13th Year] Wilmington, NC, Tuesday, 14 March 1809, page 3, column 4.

105. *From the Boston Centinel.* THE ANALYSIS Of our Public Diplomatic Dispatches, No. III. "The French decree might on the same ground be pronounced retaliation on the preceding conduct of Great Britain." See Madison's letter to Gen. **Armstrong**. The sentiment and concession contained in the foregoing extract, is full as mean, and ought to excite as general indignation as the same gentleman's declaration to Mr. **Randolph**, "France wants money and must have it." The effect of this publication of this concession will be to bar forever all our claims for redress for captures or injuries sustained under the Berlin and Milan decrees, and to furnish the French with not only pretexts but justifications for any future violations of our rights. . . Before we examine the truth of this proposition, it may be useful to consider the source of the terms used by Mr. **Madison**. The evident object of our Secretary, as well in this letter as in the late report of the committee, probably furnished by him, is to place the injuries of France and Great Britain on an equal footing; or, even further, to give a darker shade to those of the latter. . . *The Wilmington Gazette* [Number 636. 13th Year] Wilmington, NC, Tuesday, 14 March 1809, page 1, columns 1 - 3.

106. *Report of the Committee of the Legislature of Massachusetts.* {Continued from our last} The people recollected the glorious example of a former administration, and they have seen the present administration, reserving all their strength, and all of their energies, to be employed in the annihilation of that commerce which they ought to protect. By a timid and unwarranted compliance with the wishes of a foreign power, we are suddenly excluded from the ocean; our trade is destroyed; our industry paralyzed; and poverty and ruin are rapidly overspreading our land; contemplating this state of things, and recollecting their views and objects at the time of adopting the Constitution, the people do not require any further argument to convince them, that the primary objects of that compact are now neglected; that their most important interests are wantonly sacrificed, and their most essential rights flagrantly violated. . . *The Wilmington Gazette* [Number 636. 13th Year] Wilmington, NC, Tuesday, 14 March 1809, page 1, columns 2 & 3 and page 2, column 1.

107. WASHINGTON CITY, March 4, 1809. This day, at twelve o'clock, **JAMES MADISON** took the oath of Office as President of the United States, and delivered in the Chamber of the House of Representatives, in the presence of the Senate, most of the late Representatives, and large concourse of Citizens; the following SPEECH: . . . *The Wilmington Gazette* [Number 636. 13th Year] Wilmington, NC, Tuesday, 14 March 1809, page 2, columns 1 & 2.

108. One Reason is enough. The *Washington Monitor*, a violent Democratic paper, in answer to the *Aurora*, gives the following reasons why the Embargo ought to be repealed: 1. "It ought to be repealed, because it cannot be enforced." . . . These reasons, the two last of which are superfluous, recall to mind a droll circumstance which occurred sometime ago, in one of the

Pennsylvania courts, before Judge **Addison** A very important witness in a cause being called, and not answering to his name, one of his neighbors, a true son of Erin, jumped up and addressed the court. "May it please your honor, I can give you three substantial reasons why my neighbor **Patrick Dougherty**, does not attend, In the first place, he has been dead four days --" "Stop, friend, " says Addison, "you have no occasion to give any other reasons -- the first one is quite sufficient!" *The Wilmington Gazette* [Number 636. 13th Year] Wilmington, NC, Tuesday, 14 March 1809, page 2, columns 2 & 3.

109. **Rice Jones**, Esq., a member of the House of Representatives of the Indiana Territory, was deliberately murdered in the streets of Koskaskias, on the 7th of December, by Dr. **James Dunlap**.[24] Five hundred dollars are offered for the apprehending of **Dunlap**. *The Wilmington Gazette* [Number 636. 13th Year] Wilmington, NC, Tuesday, 14 March 1809, page 2, column 3.

110. For Sale, Freight or Charter, The good Ship PERSEVERANCE, lying at Mr. **H. Kelly**'s wharf. If not freighted or chartered before 12 o'clock TOMORROW, she will then be sold at Public Auction. She can be sent to sea at a very trifling expense, as her hull, sails and rigging are in complete repair. The sails and rigging are in Capt. **Hunter**'s Store. For particulars apply to the subscribers. **Z. SWAINE**. March 14. 1w. *The Wilmington Gazette* [Number 636. 13th Year] Wilmington, NC, Tuesday, 14 March 1809, page 2, column 3.

111. LOST OR MISLAID, a Note of Hand payable at the Bank for $446.32 cts. Drawn by **D. & R. Camock**, and endorsed by **James Dickson**. A reasonable reward will be given to the person who shall restore it to the subscriber. **JACOB LEVY**. March 14. 3w. *The Wilmington Gazette* [Number 636. 13th Year] Wilmington, NC, Tuesday, 14 March 1809, page 2, column 3. *The True Republican or American Whig* [Vol. 1. No. 12] Wilmington, NC, Tuesday, 21 March 1809, page 3, column 1.

112. NOTICE. THE subscriber being about leaving town requests all persons having demands against him to present their accounts for settlement. **CLEMENT STARR**. March 14. tf. *The Wilmington Gazette* [Number 636. 13th Year] Wilmington, NC, Tuesday, 14 March 1809, page 2, column 3.

113. FOR SALE, 100 Tierces of Rice, 500 Bushels of Corn, 100 M. Staves assorted, 400 M. Shingles, 500 M. feet Lumber assorted, 150 Tons timber and a few barrels of Turpentine. **A. LAZARUS**. March 14 3w. *The Wilmington Gazette* [Number 636. 13th Year] Wilmington, NC, Tuesday, 14 March 1809, page 2, column 3. *The True Republican or American Whig* [Vol. 1. No. 16] Wilmington, NC, Tuesday, 18 April 1809, page 4, column 4.

114. NOTICE, WILL be sold on Saturday the first day of April next, in Duplin County, at the late dwelling House of **Austen Bryant**, dec., all the perishable property of the said **Bryant**, yet unsold, consisting of a good horse, a yoke of oxen and cart, some hogs, cattle and sheep, and household furniture, Beds, &c. Six months credit for good notes with approved security to the administrators, who upon more begs all those having any demands against the estate to come forward on or before that day to **ISRAEL JUDGE**, *Adm'r*. March 14, 1809. 2w. *The Wilmington Gazette* [Number 636. 13th Year] Wilmington, NC, Tuesday, 14 March 1809, page 2, column 3.

115. FOR SALE. Sugar of an excellent quality in barrels, and a few bags coffee. *Also to Rent*, A Shop, and Bake-House, in Dock Street near Mr. **Dana**'s, lately in the occupation of Mr. **Jacob**

---

[24] **Rice Jones** was born in Wales on 28 September 1781. He was a graduate in medicine and law and a member of the general assembly of the Indiana Territory. He was assassinated in Kaskaskia by a political enemy on 7 December 1808. Rossiter Johnson (Ed.), *Twentieth Century Biographical Dictionary of Notable Americans*. *Vol. I-X.* (Boston MA: The Biographical Society. 1904.)

Hartman, Enquire of **JOHN LONDON**. March 14. *The Wilmington Gazette* [Number 636. 13th Year] Wilmington, NC, Tuesday, 14 March 1809, page 2, column 3.

116. To Rent, on low terms, and immediate possession given, the more lately occupied, as a book store by the subscriber, **W. S. HASELL**. March 14. *The Wilmington Gazette* [Number 636. 13th Year] Wilmington, NC, Tuesday, 14 March 1809, page 2, column 3.

117. TO RENT, AND possession given immediately that commodious House in Orange Street, lately occupied by Mr. **John MacAuslan**. For terms apply to **Wm. HATTRIDGE**. Feb. 21. *The Wilmington Gazette* [Number 636. 13th Year] Wilmington, NC, Tuesday, 14 March 1809, page 2, column 3. *The Wilmington Gazette* [Number 646. 13th Year] Wilmington, NC, Tuesday, 23 May 1809, page 1, column 2.

118. TAKEN UP by the subscriber on the 1st March 1809 [Wednesday], on the Sound near Wilmington, N.C. and committed to jail, a Mulatto fellow who says his name is **RAVIS**, and belongs to Mr. **John Jeffrey**, Union County, S.C. on Gilkings Creek. The owner is requested to come forward, prove property, pay charges, and take him away. **THOMAS JENNINGS**. March 7. tf. *The Wilmington Gazette* [Number 636. 13th Year] Wilmington, NC, Tuesday, 14 March 1809, page 2, column 3. *The Wilmington Gazette* [Number 646. 13th Year] Wilmington, NC, Tuesday, 23 May 1809, page 1, column 2.

119. *For sale at this Office*, MEMOIRS OF **WILLIAM SAMPSON**, (*Brother of Michael Sampson, of this State.*) *The Wilmington Gazette* [Number 636. 13th Year] Wilmington, NC, Tuesday, 14 March 1809, page 2, column 3.

120. *WILLIAM S. HASELL*, Has the honor of informing the public, and more particularly those persons of a literary turn, that he has received by the Venus a considerable and handsome addition to the stock of books which he before, had on hand. They are now opened and for sale at the corner of Market and Front streets, the store lately occupied by Mr. **A. Lazarus**, to which he has just removed. A Catalogue of the Books will be published in a few days. He also has for sale a variety of Stationary, Paste Board, Pencils, Sealing Wax, Wafers and Red and Black Ink Powder, &c. &c. March 14. *The Wilmington Gazette* [Number 636. 13th Year] Wilmington, NC, Tuesday, 14 March 1809, page 2, column 4.

121. NEW-YORK STATE LOTTERY, Positively commences drawing on the 12th of April next, 30,000 Dollars} Highest Prizes. A few tickets in the above Lottery for sale by **THOMAS WRIGHT**. Feb. 7. *The Wilmington Gazette* [Number 636. 13th Year] Wilmington, NC, Tuesday, 14 March 1809, page 2, column 4.

122. FOR SALE or RENT, THE house next door to the Printing Office, now occupied by Mr. **Wm. Giles**. Possession given on the first of April. Apply at this Office. February 28. *The Wilmington Gazette* [Number 636. 13th Year] Wilmington, NC, Tuesday, 14 March 1809, page 2, column 4.

123. TO RENT, That commodious slated Brick House in Front-Street and corner of Ewan's Alley. It is capable of containing two families with a kitchen to each, &c. **JOHN MARTIN**. February 7. *The Wilmington Gazette* [Number 636. 13th Year] Wilmington, NC, Tuesday, 14 March 1809, page 2, column 4.

124. 3500 bush. Turks Island Salt,[25] For sale by **JAMES FLEMING**. January 3. *The Wilmington Gazette* [Number 636. 13th Year] Wilmington, NC, Tuesday, 14 March 1809, page 2, column 4.

---

[25] Bermudians came to the Caribbean Turks and Caicos Islands in the 17th century and established what was to become the principal industry for the next 300 years - the production of salt from brine. The islands came under British colonial rule in 1766. It was Turks and Caicos salt that George Washington needed to preserve the food for his army during the American

125. NOTICE. THE subscriber requests all persons who are indebted to him by account to come forward and settle the same either by discharging or giving a note payable twelve months after the 1st January 1809; all those neglecting to come forward before the 1st February next need not expect either credit or attendance. Mr. **J. M. Henderson**, is empowered to act for the subscriber. **N. HILL**. January 3. *The Wilmington Gazette* [Number 636. 13th Year] Wilmington, NC, Tuesday, 14 March 1809, page 2, column 4.

126. NOTICE. All persons indebted to the estate of **William Grave Berry**, deceased,[26] are requested to make immediate payment, and those to whom the said estate is indebted are desired to render in their accounts attested to **Hanson Kelly**, who is authorized to settle all affairs of said estate. **James H. Ancrum**, Adm'r. Nov. 22. *The Wilmington Gazette* [Number 636. 13th Year] Wilmington, NC, Tuesday, 14 March 1809, page 2, column 4.

127. FIVE DOLLARS REWARD, RAN AWAY from the subscriber living in Wilmington a Negro Woman named **LUCY** of a yellowish complexion about 23 years of age, remarkable for her loquacity. Any person delivering said Negro to the subscriber or securing her in Wilmington jail shall be entitled to the above reward. **ALICE HERON**. Feb. 21. *The Wilmington Gazette* [Number 636. 13th Year] Wilmington, NC, Tuesday, 14 March 1809, page 2, column 4.

128. WILMINGTON, TUESDAY, MARCH 14, 1809. At last the Administration has hearkened to the voice of the people. It has been decided beyond recall, that the deleterious power of the Embargo, with all its detestable appendages, is to cease tomorrow the 15th inst. This would, indeed, be a subject of rejoicing and exceeding great joy, were it not for the intelligence of the non-intercourse, which rides the Ghost of the Embargo like an Incubus. *The Wilmington Gazette* [Number 636. 13th Year] Wilmington, NC, Tuesday, 14 March 1809, page 3, column 1.

129. A company has been formed at Edenton, N.C. for the Manufacture of Salt. *The Wilmington Gazette* [Number 636. 13th Year] Wilmington, NC, Tuesday, 14 March 1809, page 3, column 1.

130. MR. EDITOR, I have taken the liberty to address you on the subjects of the *Infamous Transparency* exhibited to public view on the evening of the fourth of March in this town, wherein a respectable portion of the union was represented in a very degrading manner, . . I am happy to find that the AUTHOR was no other than a Frenchman, who not only gave the copy but likewise furnished the funds, as appears by the declaration of Mr. **Belanger** himself, . .Inhabitants of Wilmington, are you not in honor bound to disavow the above transaction; . . An Eclipsed Yankee. *The Wilmington Gazette* [Number 636. 13th Year] Wilmington, NC, Tuesday, 14 March 1809, page 3, column 2 & 3.

131. *Communication for the Wilmington Gazette*. Mr. **T. Cowan**'s patriotic toast, "the town of Wilmington -- unanimity and friendship among its inhabitants." Among the toasts drank on the 4th March the above is selected as portraying the true American divested of party spirit, who has no object in view but the good of his country. . . LEONIDAS. *The Wilmington Gazette* [Number 636. 13th Year] Wilmington, NC, Tuesday, 14 March 1809, page 3, column 3.

132. *CYPRUS WREATH*. On Tuesday last the friends and relations of Mrs. **Elizabeth Hall**, wife of **John Hall**, Esq., assembled at Fairfield Plantation to perform to her the last sad duties of

---

Revolutionary War and that the Canadian and American fishing fleets used to salt down their catches.

[26] Died, At his plantation, *Old Town*, on the 15th inst. Mr. **William Graves Berry**. *The Wilmington Gazette* [Number 620. 12th Year] Wilmington, NC, Tuesday, 22 November 1808, page 3, column 3. Thanks to Raymond P. Fouts, *Abstracts From Newspapers of Wilmington, NC 1807-1810* (1987).

humanity by attending her obsequies . . . she now participates in the joys of the virtuous in Heaven. *The Wilmington Gazette* [Number 636. 13th Year] Wilmington, NC, Tuesday, 14 March 1809, page 3, column 4.

133. DIED In Duplin County, on the 24th February Mrs. **ELIZABETH BECK**, in the 80th year of her age. In the death of this elderly lady society has sustained a considerable loss, . . She has left a numerous progeny, to regret her death. *The Wilmington Gazette* [Number 636. 13th Year] Wilmington, NC, Tuesday, 14 March 1809, page 3, column 4.

134. *POETICAL GALAXY*. *The Wilmington Gazette* [Number 636. 13th Year] Wilmington, NC, Tuesday, 14 March 1809, page 4, column 1.

135. COFFEE. "This drink has many good physical properties, it strengthens a weak stomach, helping digestion, and the tumors and obstructions of the liver and spleen, being drank fasting for some time together. It is held in great estimation among the Egyptian and Arabian women, in common feminine cases, in which they find it does them eminent service." "Another curious particular we find mentioned here, is, that the refusing to supply a wife with Coffee is reckoned among the legal causes of a divorce in Turkey." *The Wilmington Gazette* [Number 636. 13th Year] Wilmington, NC, Tuesday, 14 March 1809, page 4, column 1.

136. *Longevity* is so frequent in *Norway*, that a clergyman in a funeral oration in that country lately lamented the *untimely* death of a *Lady*, at *seventy-four years of age*. London paper. *The Wilmington Gazette* [Number 636. 13th Year] Wilmington, NC, Tuesday, 14 March 1809, page 4, column 1.

137. The *wedding clothes*, we understand, are actually making in which Mrs. **Siddon**'s is shortly to make her appearance in the character of an *English Baroness*, for her own *Right Honorable Benefit*. *The Wilmington Gazette* [Number 636. 13th Year] Wilmington, NC, Tuesday, 14 March 1809, page 4, column 1.

138. An *Irish* print says, that Count **Kamir** in the voyage to *Greenland*, has given a *glowing* description of the mountains of *ice*. *The Wilmington Gazette* [Number 636. 13th Year] Wilmington, NC, Tuesday, 14 March 1809, page 4, column 1.

139. TAKEN UP, and now in my possession, an African man, about twenty-five years of age, five feet or nine inches high, spare made, has on a pair of plain blue trousers, a blanket & common blue Negro cap & he can scarcely be understood, from which I infer that he has been but a short time in this country:[27] he says his name is **WILL**, that his master's name is **Pee**, (being now dead,) by signs he conveys the idea his master planted cotton and corn, and that he has a cotton machine. The owner of said Negro is requested to come forward, prove his property and take him away, reasons to be assigned to the owner, why the subscribed has not committed the said Negro to jail. **JACOB LEONARD**. Brunswick County, January 17. tf. *The Wilmington Gazette* [Number 636. 13th Year] Wilmington, NC, Tuesday, 14 March 1809, page 4, column 4. *The Wilmington Gazette* [Number 646. 13th Year] Wilmington, NC, Tuesday, 23 May 1809, page 1, column 2.

140. Fifteen Dollars Reward! RAN AWAY on the 2d instant, a stout likely Negro fellow named **JACOB**, formerly the property of **Joshua Bradey**[28] deceased, quite black about six feet high,

---

[27] The importation of slaves into the United States of America was banned by Congress on 1 January 1808; but not the internal slave trade, or involvement in the international slave trade externally or the outfitting of ships for that trade by U.S. citizens.

[28] **Joshua Bradey**, also Braddy, was a planter in New Hanover County. He died in November 1807 and his will was probated in February Court 1808. **Hillory Moore** was appointed executor

plausible in conversation and very artful. He has a down look, is well known about the plantation of **Joshua Bradey**'s called Indian Creek, 8 miles from Wilmington on the North-west river. A more particular description of him will be given next week. Whosoever will apprehend the said fellow and lodge him in jail, so that I can get him, or deliver him to me in Wilmington shall receive the above reward. **HILLORY MOORE**, *Es'r*. January 31. tf. *The Wilmington Gazette* [Number 636. 13th Year] Wilmington, NC, Tuesday, 14 March 1809, page 4, column 4.

141. NOTICE, THE subscriber is anxious to close his accounts requests all those indebted to him to come forward on or before the 1st of April next, and settle their accounts either with money of by note with security, otherwise recourse to law will be had. **N. MOORE**. January 17. *The Wilmington Gazette* [Number 636. 13th Year] Wilmington, NC, Tuesday, 14 March 1809, page 4, column 4.

142. A THEFT DETECTED *And the owner called for*, FROM a Negro Woman named **Molly** I stopt about a fortnight since, 21 lbs. of Tallow. As the wench has not returned to claim it, it is probable she stole it. The person, to whom it belongs, on proving his property and paying for the advertisement, shall have it restored by calling on **THOMAS GRANDY**. February 28. 2w. *The Wilmington Gazette* [Number 636. 13th Year] Wilmington, NC, Tuesday, 14 March 1809, page 4, column 4.

143. **P. BENJAMIN** HAS the honor to inform his patrons and the public that he has removed to the house, in Market Street, lately occupied by **Edwin J. Osborne**, Esq. Where he will be ready and happy to attend any of their orders in the musical line. Having now a commodious room for the purpose, he will give lessons on the instruments he has advertised to teach, at his own house, to those who may prefer receiving them there, and he will attend those who desire it at the places they may appoint. Feb. 28. *The Wilmington Gazette* [Number 636. 13th Year] Wilmington, NC, Tuesday, 14 March 1809, page 4, column 4.

144. LIVERY STABLES. THE subscriber has established a set of Livery Stables, on the west side of Second Street, for the accommodation of those gentlemen traveling through or residing in this town, who may be disposed to avail themselves of this establishment. Every kind of grain and forage necessary for horses, shall be abundantly provided and faithfully given, and all due attention paid to them by the hostlers. The stables are quite dry& shall be furnished with litter every evening. **WM. WILLKINGS**. Feb. 28. *The Wilmington Gazette* [Number 636. 13th Year] Wilmington, NC, Tuesday, 14 March 1809, page 4, column 4. *The Wilmington Gazette* [Number 646. 13th Year] Wilmington, NC, Tuesday, 23 May 1809, page 1, column 2.

145. *WILMINGTON, N.C.* PRINTED AND PUBLISHED BY *WILLIAM S. HASELL*. CONDITIONS, 1. THREE DOLLARS a year, payable in advance, or FOUR DOLLARS if not paid within the first six months. 2. No subscription can be received for a less time than SIX MONTHS. 3. No paper will be discontinued until arrearages are settled, unless the accounts be put in suit. *The Wilmington Gazette* [Number 636. 13th Year] Wilmington, NC, Tuesday, 14 March 1809, page 4, column 4. *The Wilmington Gazette* [Number 646. 13th Year] Wilmington, NC, Tuesday, 23 May 1809, page 4, column 4.

146. WASHINGTON CITY, MARCH 3. THIS day will form a bright æra on the page of history. Never will it be forgotten as long as liberty is dear to man, that it was on this day that **THOMAS JEFFERSON** retired from the supreme magistracy amidst the blessings and regrets of millions. *The True Republican or American Whig* [Vol. 1. No. 12] Wilmington, NC, Tuesday, 21 March 1809, page 1, column 1.

147. *NOTICE*. THE Subscribers have obtained letters of Administration upon the Estate of Col. **William Jones**, deceased. Late of New Hanover County -- All person indebted to his Estate, are requested to make payment -- and those who have demand upon the same are required to present

---

of the will. New Hanover County Will Book AB, page 166. Thanks to Mae B. Graves, *New Hanover County Abstracts of Wills* (Old New Hanover Genealogical Society: 1981, reprinted 1999).

them within the time limited by an Act of the General Assembly, in such cases made and provided. ***John Colvin, William Jones Larkins.*** } Adm'rs. March 18, 1809. *The True Republican or American Whig* [Vol. 1. No. 12] Wilmington, NC, Tuesday, 21 March 1809, page 3, column 1.

148. PRICES CURRENT. *WILMINGTON, MARCH 21*, 1809.

Merchandize	quan rated	from D C.	to D C.
Bacon,	*Lb*	9	10
Butter,		18	20
Beeswax,		33	
Beef,	*Bbl*	9	10
Brandy 4th proof,	*Gal*	2 50	2 75
Corn,	*Bush*	56	60
Cotton, Upland	*Lb*	15	16
[tear in film]			
Coffee,		30	
Flour,	*Bbt*	7 50	8
Flaxseed,	*Gask*	7 50	8
Gin, American	*Gal*	75	
Lumber, pine			
Boards 1 1-4 inch	th. Ft	9	10
Scantling,		8	8 50
Timber, sq'r pine	40 ft	2 50	
Shingles, Cypress	thou	1 25	1 50
Staves, w o Hhds		20	25
k o ditto		9	9 50
w o bbls.		10	10 50
Heading w o hhd		28	30
Lard,	*Lb*	10	12
Molasses,	*Gal*	50	60
Naval Stores,			
Tar 32 Gallons,	*Bbl*	1 50	1 75
Rosin,		2 50	
Turpentine,			
320 lbs gross,		3	3 25
Spir. Turpentine,	*Gal*	37	40
Pork,	*Bbl*	13	14
Peas,	*Bush*	58	62
Rum Jamaica}	*Gal*	1 50	
4th proof,			
3d proof,		1 25	
American ditto,		70	
Rice,	100 b	2 75	3
Salt,	*Bush*	75	
Liverpool		70	
Sugar Muscovado,	100 b	11	13
Loaf,	*Ll*	21	22
Tobacco,	100 *lb*	4	4 50

The True Republican or American Whig [Vol. 1. No. 12] Wilmington, NC, Tuesday, 21 March 1809, page 3, column 1. See slight changes in prices in these issues of *The True Republican or American Whig* [Vol. 1. No. 16] Wilmington, NC, Tuesday, 18 April 1809, page 1, column 1; *The True Republican or American Whig* [Vol. 1. No. 18] Wilmington, NC, Tuesday, 2 May 1809, page 1, column 1; *The True Republican or American Whig* [Vol. 1. No. 19] Wilmington, NC, Tuesday, 9 May 1809, page 1, column 1; *The True Republican or American Whig* [Vol. 1. No. 20] Wilmington,

NC, Tuesday, 16 May 1809, page 1, column 1; *The True Republican or American Whig* [Vol. 1. No. 21] Wilmington, NC, Tuesday, 23 May 1809, page 1, column 1; *The Wilmington Gazette* [Number 646. 13th Year] Wilmington, NC, Tuesday, 23 May 1809, page 3, column 4. *The True Republican or American Whig* [Vol. 1. No. 23] Wilmington, NC, Tuesday, 6 June 1809, page 1, column 1. *The True Republican or American Whig* [Vol. 1. No. 25] Wilmington, NC, Tuesday, 20 June 1809, page 1, column 1. *The True Republican or American Whig* [Vol. 1. No. 27] Wilmington, NC, Tuesday, 4 July 1809, page 1, column 1. *The True Republican or American Whig* [Vol. 1. No. 45] Wilmington, NC, Tuesday, 7 November 1809, page 3, column 3.

149. On Friday the 17th instant, a few sons and descendents of St. PATRICK partook of a dinner prepared by Mr. **Dick**, in honor of the day -- when the following toasts were drank, and the evening passed in an agreeable and convivial manner. 1. The glorious and immortal memory of St. Patrick. 2. The Mother of all Saints. 3. ERIN -- has the deserved reproach for daring to be free? . . 17. The American and Irish Fair. *The True Republican or American Whig* [Vol. 1. No. 12] Wilmington, NC, Tuesday, 21 March 1809, page 3, column 2.

150. VOLUNTEERS. *By the President* - Destruction to all parties in the United States, except that party whose object is to maintain the honor and independence of the country. *By the Vice-President* - Our friends in Ireland -- As they cannot be free, may they endeavor to be contented. *By Mr. T. Cowan* - The trade and navigation of the Cape Fear. *By Mr. Howell* - The Cincinnatus of America, **Charles Cotesworth Pinckney**. *By Mr. Hobbs* - May the majority govern as they wish to be govern. *By Mr. John Usher* - The two great contending parties in the United States, . . may they seek to cultivate friendship and harmony with each other. *The True Republican or American Whig* [Vol. 1. No. 12] Wilmington, NC, Tuesday, 21 March 1809, page 3, column 2.

151. COMMUNICATION. Messrs. Editors. The chagrin and unbounded hatred of a few, can always be excited to madness, by the happy declaration -- Madison is our President. A writer in the *Gazette* of the last week, with all the shameless effrontery of pampered impudence, makes his remarks upon the splendid display of Republicanism as exhibited on the fourth of March, in honor of our present Chief Magistrate, and terms it emphatically, an *Infamous Transparency*. . . I call upon you, "Eclipsed Yankee," to answer the following question: Are you not a native of England? I believe, proof the most satisfactory, can be adduced, to show, that you are not only an Englishman, but that in addition, you are an officious meddler -- a deceited advocate of the British, and a continual riveter of the American government. *A pretty fellow, indeed, to talk about French Influence!* DETECTOR. *The True Republican or American Whig* [Vol. 1. No. 12] Wilmington, NC, Tuesday, 21 March 1809, page 3, columns 2 & 3.

152. Highly Important News! To the politeness of Capt. **CONNELLY** who arrived here on Sunday, after a very short passage from Charleston, we are indebted for the following interesting intelligence, contained in the *City Gazette* of the 18th instant. *The True Republican or American Whig* [Vol. 1. No. 12] Wilmington, NC, Tuesday, 21 March 1809, page 3, columns 3 & 4.

153. *CURIOUS MARRIAGE*. Married, in Connecticut, lately, Mr. **Samual Saunders,** a widower, aged 97, to Miss **Susanna Bailard**, aged 85 years. The parties have never seen each other and probably never will! *The True Republican or American Whig* [Vol. 1. No. 12] Wilmington, NC, Tuesday, 21 March 1809, page 3, column 4.

154. Married. At Newbern, Mr. **Thomas M'Lin**, merchant, to Miss **Eliza Beitner** -- At the same place, Mr. **Henry M. Cooke**, merchant, to Miss **Frances Buxton**. In Duplin, on the 13th inst. **Daniel L. Kenan** Esq., Sheriff of that county, to Miss **Mary James**. In the same county on the 15th, **James Holmes** Esq., Sheriff of Sampson, to Miss **Sarah Norman**. *The True Republican or American Whig* [Vol. 1. No. 12] Wilmington, NC, Tuesday, 21 March 1809, page 3, column 4.

155. Speech DELIVERED BY MR. **J. G. JACKSON** in the House of Representatives of the United States, On the motion for raising the Embargo, and authorizing letters of marquee and

reprisal. *The True Republican or American Whig* [Vol. 1. No. 16] Wilmington, NC, Tuesday, 18 April 1809, page 1, column 1 through page 2, column 3.

156. President Adam's letter. Office of the Anti-Monarchist, March 20, 1809. The following letter of the late President of the United States, the venerable patriot, **JOHN ADAMS**, was addressed to **Daniel Wright** and **Erastus Lyman**, Esquires of Northampton, Massachusetts, in answer to a letter dated March 8, 1809, which they addressed to him, at the desire of the Republicans of that town, requesting him to express his opinion respecting the present circumstances of the nation, with regard to foreign powers, and domestic parties, -- Mr. Adams' letter was dated Quincy, March 13, & has the postmark of the Quincy post office, and franked by Mr. Adams. The original is left at the post office, for the inspection of those who wish to see it. *The True Republican or American Whig* [Vol. 1. No. 16] Wilmington, NC, Tuesday, 18 April 1809, page 2, columns 3 and 4.

157. LATE FOREIGN NEWS! London, February 5. There is no doubt that three bills have passed the American Legislature; the bill for enforcing the embargo -- the non-intercourse bill, and a bill prohibiting American vessels from sailing under foreign licenses. These measures are extremely well calculated to complete what the embargo began, and bring to utter ruin the American commerce. February 6. Bonaparte has communicated to the Senate his resolution respecting Spain and Portugal; the latter is to be united to Spain, and to form a new kingdom for his brother Joseph: in compensation whereof, Biscay, the rest of Navarre, part of Aragon, and Catalonia, are to be annexed to France; and the river Ebro, from Sandere to Tortosa, is said to be the future limit of France. February 7. The latest account from Portugal have been received by a vessel which left Lisbon on the 27th ult. The French has not then reached the capital. February 8. A vessel has arrived from San Lucar, in the vicinity of Cadiz. It appears that the exertions were continued in the South of Spain for the public defense, and that the Junta was active in diffusing among the people a spirit suited to meet the exigencies of the times, and favorable expectations were entertained of the result of their endeavors. February 9. The intelligence of the continuance of the American embargo, has caused great sensation in the north of Germany, where colonial produce has become very scarce. *The True Republican or American Whig* [Vol. 1. No. 16] Wilmington, NC, Tuesday, 18 April 1809, page 3, column 1.

158. Philadelphia, April 5. WHAT NEXT? The Federalists of the East are gradually drawing the curtain which conceals their designs. The address of the legislature to the people of Massachusetts, is a most instructive document, in this address, the people are called upon to unite their strength against the administration; to elect a *federal governor*, in order that there may be a perfect coalition between the difference branches of the state government, and that the whole power may be in the hands of the Federalists -- hints are darkly thrown out of some ulterior measures to be adopted by the party, for whose accomplishments this coalition may be necessary -- every art is used to excite the eastern against the southern states -- the latter are impudently charged with a hostility to commerce, and every exertion is used to set the farmers of the East against the planters of the South. These circumstances disclose the scheme of a 'Northern Confederacy,' to be composed of the New England states and Vermont. **Timothy Pickering**'s toast, at New York, proves his anxiety to connect the state of N. York in this ominous project. *Enquirer*. *The True Republican or American Whig* [Vol. 1. No. 16] Wilmington, NC, Tuesday, 18 April 1809, page 3, columns 2 and 3.

159. The True Republican. Wilmington, Tuesday, April 18, 1809. His Britannic majesty's sloop of war Rosamond, Capt. **Walker**, arrived at Norfolk on the 3d of this month; in 41 days from Falmouth, with dispatches for Mr. **Erskine**. London papers to the 9th of February, were received at Washington City, brought by this vessel. . . New York prints of the 6th of April, mentions the arrival of the British packet, which sailed from Falmouth on the 21st of February, and some days

later than the sloop of war which arrived at Norfolk. The packet brings out a Spanish minister, and his secretary, from the Central Junta. A London paper received at New York says, 'Dispatches of considerable importance are immediately to be sent out to Mr. **Erskine**, our minister in America. It is confidently stated that they will communicate the determination of our government to withdraw our orders in council, provided the government of the United States shall consent to specific conditions, chiefly of a commercial nature. The gentleman who is to be charged with these dispatches is a Mr. **Oakley**. The *National Intelligencer* of the 10th instant says, Mr. **Charles Oakley**, secretary of Legation of his Britannic Majesty to the United States, arrived in this city on Friday last. *The True Republican or American Whig* [Vol. 1. No. 16] Wilmington, NC, Tuesday, 18 April 1809, page 3, column 3.

160. The Commissioners of this State, says the *Raleigh Register*, for adjusting the disputed boundary with South Carolina are we understand to meet the Commissioners on the part of that State, in the course of the present month, for the purpose of running the boundary line (heretofore agreed upon) between the two States. General **John Moore** having resigned his appointment, General **Montford Stokes** has been named in his place. Dr. **Joseph Caldwell** has been appointed Astronomer to the commission. *The True Republican or American Whig* [Vol. 1. No. 16] Wilmington, NC, Tuesday, 18 April 1809, page 3, column 3.

161. *Extract of a letter from Savannah, dated March 17.* "The governor of Florida[29] has laid a duty on imports of -- percent and exports of 6 percent, which have caused some agents to leave Amelia Island: from which place the captains of vessels must go to St. Augustine to enter and clear, a distance of a hundred miles. *The True Republican or American Whig* [Vol. 1. No. 16] Wilmington, NC, Tuesday, 18 April 1809, page 3, column 3.

162. DIED, At his seat in Richmond County, on the 31st ultimo, in the 62d year of his age General **Henry W. Harrington**. He was an active and useful officer, and acquired honor in the revolution which secured to this country its independence. In private life he percified all the virtues that recommend a montour confidence & regard; the nicest sense of honor & the strictest principles of justice marked every transaction of his life. *The True Republican or American Whig* [Vol. 1. No. 16] Wilmington, NC, Tuesday, 18 April 1809, page 3, column 4.

163. DIED, On the 23d ultimo, in Orange County, (Virginia,) Mr. **John Madison**, nephew of the President of the United States. *The True Republican or American Whig* [Vol. 1. No. 16] Wilmington, NC, Tuesday, 18 April 1809, page 3, column 4.

164. Marine List. PORT OF WILMINGTON. Entered. Sch'r Rover, **Whitby**, New River. Sch'r Telegraph, **Nelson**, Charleston. Sloop Francesco de Pawlo, **Gomez**, Havannah. Sch'r Eagle, **Goodvine**, New River. Sch'r Polly, **Jarvis**, Topsail Sd. Sch'r Aurora, **Davis**, Charleston. Cleared. Sch'r Regulator, **McIlhenny**, Charleston. Brig Clarisa, **McLean**, Amelia Island. Ship Perseverance, **Owen**, St. Bartholomew. Brig Paul Hamilton, **Hailey**, Charleston. *The True Republican or American Whig* [Vol. 1. No. 16] Wilmington, NC, Tuesday, 18 April 1809, page 3, column 4.

165. NOTICE, MY Wife **HANNAH**, has deserted my Bed and Board, without any provocation. I do hereby forward all person whatever, from dealing with her, as I am determined not to pay, or answer any of her contracts, to which I request all persons to take due notice. Nevertheless, if my said wife **Hannah** will return to me, I will support her as usual, or procure a good house for her reception. **MOSES RITTER**. April 17, 1809. *The True Republican or American Whig* [Vol. 1. No. 16] Wilmington, NC, Tuesday, 18 April 1809, page 3, column 4. *The True Republican or American Whig* [Vol. 1. No. 18]

---

[29] During the Second Spanish Period of Florida 1784 - 1821, the Governor of East Florida was **Enrique White** from 1796 - 1811. He died 13 April 1811. Thanks to C. Mack Wills, *St. John's County Deaths* (St. Augustine Genealogical Society: 2006).

Wilmington, NC, Tuesday, 2 May 1809, page 4, column 4. [April 20.] *The True Republican or American Whig* [Vol. 1. No. 20] Wilmington, NC, Tuesday, 16 May 1809, page 3, column 1. *The True Republican or American Whig* [Vol. 1. No. 21] Wilmington, NC, Tuesday, 23 May 1809, page 4, column 3.

166. Account of a dead body found under the porch of Christ Church in Boston, Massachusetts, in a high state of preservation. The ground under the porch of the entrance of the church was directed to be dug up. At a distance of 6 feet from the surface, a grave was discovered, in which was found a coffin of hard pitch pine, commonly called the Norway pine, which on being opened, contained another of the same wood. Both coffins had on their lids, in brass nails, the letters J. T. and gravestone at the head of the grave, declared the person interred there, to be Mr. **John Thomas** of the island of Barbados, aged 45 years, who died 24th June. A.D. 1726. *The True Republican or American Whig* [Vol. 1. No. 16] Wilmington, NC, Tuesday, 18 April 1809, page 4, column 2.

167. DIVISION ORDERS, OFFICERS commanding the second and third Brigades will issue immediate orders for causing the Troops of the counties, hereinafter mentioned to be paraded completely prepared for review at their respective courthouses, precisely at 12 o'clock on the following days, of May next; Duplin county, on Thursday, the 11th day. Craven County, on Saturday, the 12th. Beaufort County, on Tuesday, the 16th day. Hyde County, on Thursday, the 18th day. Carteret County, on Tuesday, the 23d day. Onslow County, on Thursday, the 25th day. The utmost punctuality is expected, and field returns are to be made to the commanding officer within one hour after the review. By order of Major General **Smith, J. W. LEONARD**, A.D.C. Belvedere, March 30. 3w. *The True Republican or American Whig* [Vol. 1. No. 16] Wilmington, NC, Tuesday, 18 April 1809, page 4, column 2. *The True Republican or American Whig* [Vol. 1. No. 18] Wilmington, NC, Tuesday, 2 May 1809, page 4, column 4.

168. WANTED, ONE hundred thousand White Oak BARREL STAVES, for which CASH will be paid on delivery, *Apply to* **BURGWIN & ORME**, April 4. tf. *The True Republican or American Whig* [Vol. 1. No. 16] Wilmington, NC, Tuesday, 18 April 1809, page 4, column 2. *The True Republican or American Whig* [Vol. 1. No. 18] Wilmington, NC, Tuesday, 2 May 1809, page 4, column 4. *The True Republican or American Whig* [Vol. 1. No. 20] Wilmington, NC, Tuesday, 16 May 1809, page 4, column 4. *The True Republican or American Whig* [Vol. 1. No. 21] Wilmington, NC, Tuesday, 23 May 1809, page 4, column 4. *The True Republican or American Whig* [Vol. 1. No. 23] Wilmington, NC, Tuesday, 6 June 1809, page 1, column 1.

169. LIST OF LETTERS, *Remaining in the Post Office at this place.* Col. **Samuel Ashe**, 2; **Stephen Anthony, William Atkins, William Bloodworth, John Befunt, Daniel Bellune**, 2; **Cyrus Bryant**, 2; **Stephen Bellugs, Thos. Bishop, John C. Brown, John Beasley, Benjamin Ballard, G. Brown, Joshua L. Baker, James Collins, William Cooper, Ch'ls Carroll**, Capt. **T. Childs**, 8; **Jonah Clarke, Adam Cotton, Peter Carpenter, T. Clements**, Miss **R. Church**, Captain **Nicholas Darrell**, 2; **J. Dyer**, 2; Messrs. **Hannahan & Davison**, Capt. **Thomas Day, Stephen B. Daniel, Wm. Davidson**, 2; **Jas. Downing, Alexander Dickson, Alex'r Delgairnes**, 8; **George Duncan**, Doct. **R. Everitt, J. Ellingwood, Edward Franklin, John Freeman, George Gillespie**, 2; **Aaron Gomez**, 2; **Nathaniel Guyteer & Co., Geo. Glassen, J. Goulden, William S. Handy, James Huse, P. Hodges, William Harris, Cornelius Hurst, Abner Hopton**, 2; **Benj. Hall**, 2; **William Hall, A. Hall**, 2; **Elie Howard, Jeremiah Buckhannon, John Hegrose, William Hubbel, Robert Howe, Jacques Jones, William W. Jones, Joseph Jacobs, Jeremiah Johnson, Nancy Johnson**, Capt. **Herman Klevenhausen, John Laws**, Miss **Betsy Livingston, Robert Lowry**, 4; **Maclin Lee, Nathan B. Lefton, Jeremiah Lesters, Ezekiel Lane, John M'Cole, Jas. Miller, Henry Minot, Wm. B. Mumford**, Mrs. **Musgroves**, Capt. **Alexander Morgan, William Miller, William M'Keel**, Miss **Catharine M'Cole**, Mrs. **Marshall**, Capt. **Nettles, James Newton, Richard Nixon, Alexander Petenson**, 2; **William Poutnap, Thomas Parke, James Parke, John Patterson, Solomon Pennicke**, Capt. **Wm. Price**, Mrs. **Reinhold, Wm. W. Rodman**, 4; **James Redmond**, Capt. **Thomas Russ, Joseh Russ, Sempronius Russ**, 2; **N. W. Ruggles**, 2; **Alexander Russell, John G. Scull**, 6; Sheriff of

New Hanover **Sam'l Swann, Jenriet Spendlove, William Smith, Ephraim Sutton, John Swann, Thomas Sweney, John Smith,** Capt. **Richard Sears, William Selby, James Vaughan, John Wilkings, Mares Wilson, Edward Ward, John Woistwick, Joseph Wicker,** 2; **Joseph White,** 2; **Eluathan Wood, Jonathan Wood, Elizabeth Waters, Thomas Wright,** 2; Rev. **Moses Waddle, Chloe Warton, Wm. Wilkinson, Wm. Mosely, David Walker, Thomas B. Wilkinson, Lott Williams, James R. Wisbee, Christopher Wallace,** 2; Miss **Younger,** 2. J. **LORD,** P. M. April 4. 3w. *The True Republican or American Whig* [Vol. 1. No. 16] Wilmington, NC, Tuesday, 18 April 1809, page 4, column 3.

170. TEN DOLLARS REWARD. RANAWAY, TWO Apprentice Boys by the names of ***JOHN GIVEN*** AND ***BARNEY WHARFFS***, they are about 19 years of age; the latter speaks broken English. If found thirty miles from Wilmington a reasonable expense will be paid to lodge them in jail or onboard the ship Cora, at the flats. I also forewarn all masters of vessels and other persons from shipping or harboring them, under the penalty of the law. ***GEO. MOONEY.*** *April* 11. 3t. *The True Republican or American Whig* [Vol. 1. No. 16] Wilmington, NC, Tuesday, 18 April 1809, page 4, column 3. *The True Republican or American Whig* [Vol. 1. No. 18] Wilmington, NC, Tuesday, 2 May 1809, page 4, column 4.

171. RANAWAY FROM the Subscriber, in Wilmington, two Negro Men, ***JACK & PETER***, **JACK** is a Cooper, and formerly belonged to **Joseph Scott**, deceased, of Sampson County; he is about 38 years of age, 5 feet, 8 inches high, stout made and looks well; he has a scar on the side of his nose, and the lower part of on Ear bit off in fighting. It is probable he will be lurking about the North east River, between the Big and Little Bridges, or at Mr. **T. Larkins** on Long Creek, as he has a wife there. -- **PETER** is between 30 and 40 years of age, about 5 feet, 9 inches high, very stout made, and quite black. I expect he will lurk about town, or perhaps, may endeavor to get to Fayetteville, as he was once owned by **James Beggs**, and waggoned for him, or to Raleigh, where he was owned by **James Meares**. A reward of five dollars for each, if taken without the County, or double, if taken without it, will be paid to any person, who will lodge then in the Wilmington jail. I do hereby forbid all persons from harbouring or employing in any way whatever, the said Negroes, **Jack** and **Peter** and particularly caution master of vessels against carrying them away, or suffering their crews to conceal them, as the law will be rigidly enforced against such offenders. ***SAMUEL NOBLE.*** *April* 2. *The True Republican or American Whig* [Vol. 1. No. 16] Wilmington, NC, Tuesday, 18 April 1809, page 4, column 3.

172. MERCURY, Is a beautiful chestnut coloured HORSE, well marked, fifteen hands and a half high, capital movements, and of uncommon bottom. PEDIGREE, MERCURY was got by the imported horse *Driver*, his dam by the imported horse *Eclipse*, the sire of the famous horse *Nantoka*, and other capital runners; his grand dam by the famous horse *Union*, his great grand dam by the imported old *Traveller*, out of old *Selima*, by the *Godolphin Arabian*.

☞ The above horse stands at the Subscribers stable, in Brunswick County, ten miles from Wilmington, at twelve dollars and a half the season, and twenty dollars to ensure. Excellent pasturage gratis, and every necessary attention paid to mares during their continuance with the Horses. Such persons as with their mares fed with corn, can be accommodated at the customary price. **WILLIAM WINGATE.** March 31. tf. *The True Republican or American Whig* [Vol. 1. No. 16] Wilmington, NC, Tuesday, 18 April 1809, page 4, column 4. *The True Republican or American Whig* [Vol. 1. No. 18] Wilmington, NC, Tuesday, 2 May 1809, page 3, column 3. *The True Republican or American Whig* [Vol. 1. No. 19] Wilmington, NC, Tuesday, 9 May 1809, page 4, column 4. *The True Republican or American Whig* [Vol. 1. No. 20] Wilmington, NC, Tuesday, 16 May 1809, page 4, column 4. *The True Republican or American Whig* [Vol. 1. No. 21] Wilmington, NC, Tuesday, 23 May 1809, page 4, column 4; *The True Republican or American Whig* [Vol. 1. No. 23] Wilmington, NC, Tuesday, 6 June 1809, page 1, column 1. *The True Republican or American Whig* [Vol. 1. No. 25] Wilmington, NC, Tuesday, 20 June 1809, page 4, column 4.

173. NOTICE. THE Subscribers having entered into business under the firm of **BURGWIN** and **ORME** offer for sale at the Store lately occupied by Mr. **David Smith** and extensive assortment of HARDWARE & SHIP CHANDLERY. **Geo. W. B. Burgwin. James Orme**. March 28. 4w.
The True Republican or American Whig [Vol. 1. No. 16] Wilmington, NC, Tuesday, 18 April 1809, page 4, column 4.

174. FOR SALE,
    70 Boxes Brown Sugar
    24 do White do.
    6 Hhds Muscovado do.
    20 Bbls best green Coffee
    2 Pipes 4th proof Gin
    1 do. Lisbon Wine
    40 Hhds. Molasses
    12 kegs Virginia Manufactured tobacco
    18 Pieces Russian Duck
    8 do. Ravens do.
    70 Boxes Soap
    6 do. Chocolate
    3000 Bushels Turks Island Salt
    4 Trunks Calicoes, assorted
    3000 lbs. Codfish
    1,200,000 Feet& 1.4 Inch Boards
    300,000 Shingles
    20,000 Red Oak hhds Staves.
HANSON KELLY. April 2. tf. *The True Republican or American Whig* [Vol. 1. No. 16] Wilmington, NC, Tuesday, 18 April 1809, page 4, column 3. *The True Republican or American Whig* [Vol. 1. No. 19] Wilmington, NC, Tuesday, 9 May 1809, page 4, column 4. *The True Republican or American Whig* [Vol. 1. No. 20] Wilmington, NC, Tuesday, 16 May 1809, page 4, column 4. *The True Republican or American Whig* [Vol. 1. No. 21] Wilmington, NC, Tuesday, 23 May 1809, page 4, column 4. *The Wilmington Gazette* [Number 646. 13th Year] Wilmington, NC, Tuesday, 23 May 1809, page 1, column 1. *The True Republican or American Whig* [Vol. 1. No. 23] Wilmington, NC, Tuesday, 6 June 1809, page 4, column 4. *The True Republican or American Whig* [Vol. 1. No. 25] Wilmington, NC, Tuesday, 20 June 1809, page 4, column 3. *The True Republican or American Whig* [Vol. 1. No. 27] Wilmington, NC, Tuesday, 4 July 1809, page 4, column 4.

175. DESERTED FROM my Company of Artilleries, on the night of the 19th instant, **John Hinson** and **William Cox**. **Hinson** is a native of North Carolina, five feet six inches and one half high, twenty two years of age; has blue eyes, light hair, fair complexion; by occupation a carriage maker. **William Cox** is a Virginian, six feet high, twenty six years of age; has blue eyes, light hair, ruddy complexion; by occupation a hatter. Fifty Dollars reward will be paid for securing the above deferrers in any jail, and information given to me; or if delivered to any commissioned officer in the army of the United States, the expenses will be paid independent of the reward.
ADDISON B. ARMISTEAD, Captain, 1st Reg. U. S. Artilleries, Commanding. Savannah, March 20. *The True Republican or American Whig* [Vol. 1. No. 16] Wilmington, NC, Tuesday, 18 April 1809, page 4, column 4. *The True Republican or American Whig* [Vol. 1. No. 18] Wilmington, NC, Tuesday, 2 May 1809, page 4, column 4.

176. MR. **F. J. BELANGER**, Has the honor of informing the parents and guardians of young ladies and gentlemen, who are desirous to learn to speak and write the French language, that having concluded to remain some time longer in Wilmington, he will be happy to devote a part of his time to that kind of instruction. He also purposes to teach Latin Grammar. His terms may be known by applying at his house. April 10. *The True Republican or American Whig* [Vol. 1. No. 16] Wilmington, NC, Tuesday, 18 April 1809, page 4, column 4. *The True Republican or American Whig* [Vol. 1. No. 18] Wilmington, NC, Tuesday, 2 May 1809, page 4, column 4. *The Wilmington Gazette* [Number 646. 13th Year] Wilmington, NC, Tuesday, 23 May 1809, page 1, column 2.

177. CORRESPONDENCE, Between the Ministers of Russia, France and England, on the subject of a GENERAL PEACE. No. I. Letter from Count **Nicholas de Romanzoff** to Mr. Secretary [**George**] **Canning**, date Erfurth, September 30, (Oct. 12). Received October 21. . . No. II. Letter from his majesty the emporer of the Russias, and **Bonaparte**, to his majesty, dated Erfurth, 12th of October, 1808. Received 21st October. . . No. III. Letter from M. **de Champagny** to Mr. Secretary **Canning**, dated Erfurth, 12th Oct., 1808. Received Oct 21st. . . No. IV. The inclosure No. IV., is verbatim the same as No. II. The joint letter of **Alexander** and **Napolean**, except that this letter, which is transformed by the French minister, is signed **Napolean - Alexander**. In the one letter **Alexander** signed first, in the other **Napolean**. No. V. Letters from Secretary **Canning** to the Russian ambassador at Paris, dated Foreign Office, 28th Oct. 1808. . . No. VI. Letter from Mr. Secretary **Canning** to M. **de Champagny**, dated Foreign Office, 21st October 1808. . . No. VII. OFFICIAL NOTE. . . No. VIII. Translation -- Note. . . *The True Republican or American Whig* [Vol. 1. No. 18] Wilmington, NC, Tuesday, 2 May 1809, page 1, columns 1 - 4 & page 2, columns 1 -2.

178. New-York, April 15. LATEST SPANISH NEWS AND DIRECT FROM SPAIN. By a passenger in the ship Thomas Jefferson, Captain **Morrison**, from Spain, we have received intelligence from that quarter to the 28th February. We are sorry to say they are such as leave but little doubt that ere now the whole of that deluded country is in the possession of the French, excepting Cadiz & probably some other place in Andalusia and Grenada. *The True Republican or American Whig* [Vol. 1. No. 18] Wilmington, NC, Tuesday, 2 May 1809, page 2, column 2.

179. WEST-INDIES. *Extract of a letter to the Editor of the Mercantile Advertiser, from a correspondent at Havana.* "March 21. At 12 o'clock this day, two Frenchmen from this country were mobbed all the way from the gates of the government house. It appears that this was the signal for a general attack upon all the French inhabitants; for in half an hour three great mobs of Negroes and mulattos, to the number of 6 of 7000, paraded the principal streets, armed with clubs and stones, wreaking their fury upon every house which they suspected to contain a Frenchman, destroying furniture and liquors, and sparing neither age nor sex. *The True Republican or American Whig* [Vol. 1. No. 18] Wilmington, NC, Tuesday, 2 May 1809, page 3, column 3.

180. Captain **Tatem** from St. Croix, arrived at Boston, informs that an insurrection had occurred at Guadeloupe in favor of the British, and an expedition was proceeding against the island, and that the Spaniards had gone against the city of St. Domingo. *The True Republican or American Whig* [Vol. 1. No. 18] Wilmington, NC, Tuesday, 2 May 1809, page 2, column 3.

181. On the night of the 21st instant, a most horrid and deliberate Murder was committed at Raleigh, on the body of Mr. **Patrick Conway**, merchant of that place. He had spent the evening with a few of his friends at a house within a short distance of his own, and at 10 o'clock returned to his store, where he usually slept. In a short time afterwards an alarm was given by two persons passing by the store, that the front door was open and that Mr. **Conway** was heard to groan, as if much distress. He was accordingly found weltering in blood behind the counter, and his head and face shockingly disfigured with wounds. A young man of the name of **Owen** was suspicioned the next morning and taken into custody -- after an examination of several witnesses, he was committed to jail, to be tried before the next Fall Superior Court at Raleigh. Mr. **Conway** was a native of Ireland, and had resided in Raleigh about two years, much respected by the inhabitants. *The True Republican or American Whig* [Vol. 1. No. 18] Wilmington, NC, Tuesday, 2 May 1809, page 3, column 3.

182. It is stated, on the authority of advices from Bermuda, that a frigate had arrived from England, bringing instructions to the admiral commanding on the West India station, not to molest American vessels or property. *Philadelphia paper*. *The True Republican or American Whig* [Vol. 1. No. 18] Wilmington, NC, Tuesday, 2 May 1809, page 3, column 4.

183. Marine List. PORT OF WILMINGTON. ENTERED. Ship Perseverance, **Bowman**, New York. Sch'r Polly, **Jarvis**, Swansborough. Sch'r Rebecca, **Smith**, Boston. Sch'r Comet, **Jenkins**, New York. Sch'r Resolution, **Beats**, Boston. CLEARED. Sch'r P. D. Experiment, **Pearsons**, Charleston. Sch'r Amanda, **Swain**, Amelia Island. Sch'r Little John, --------, N. River. Sch'r Revenge, **Barton**, Barbadoes. Sch'r Sally & Betty, **Haws**, Boston. Sch'r R. Prosperis, **Goidoux**, St. Barth'ws. Schr' Three Sisters, -------, Chalreston. *The True Republican or American Whig* [Vol. 1. No. 18] Wilmington, NC, Tuesday, 2 May 1809, page 3, column 4.

184. Supplementary DIVISION ORDERS. IT having been represented that such delays may probably arise from the state of the Roads and Ferries, as to render more time necessary for arrival at some of the Counties than has been allowed in the Division Orders of the 30th March; the following alterations have been adopted, of which the proper officers will take and give due notice. The Review in Craven County on Saturday the 20th. In Carteret on Wednesday the 24th. In Onslow on Friday the 25th} Of May next.

☞ THE Commanding Officers of Brunswick, New-Hanover, Pitt, Lenoir, Greene, Johnston and Wayne, will have their Regiments in readiness to be reviewed in the course of a few months. By order of Major General **Smith**. *JACOB LEONARD*, A.D.C. Belvedere, April 21, 1809. 2w. *The True Republican or American Whig* [Vol. 1. No. 18] Wilmington, NC, Tuesday, 2 May 1809, page 3, column 4. *The True Republican or American Whig* [Vol. 1. No. 19] Wilmington, NC, Tuesday, 9 May 1809, page 3, column 4.

185. **LEWIS PERRET**, WATCH-MAKER, INFORMS the inhabitants of Wilmington, that he intends carrying on the business of WATCH-MAKING, & c. and has taken the house lately occupied by Mr. **Canu**. Those Gentlemen who may think proper to encourage him in the above business, may reply upon having their work done in the best manner, and on moderate terms. May 1. 2w. *The True Republican or American Whig* [Vol. 1. No. 18] Wilmington, NC, Tuesday, 2 May 1809, page 3, column 4. *The True Republican or American Whig* [Vol. 1. No. 19] Wilmington, NC, Tuesday, 9 May 1809, page 3, column 4.

186. *Biography of FLORIDA BLANCA*. On the 20th of December died in this city aged 81 years and 2 months, his Excellency don **JOSEPH MONNINO**, count of Florida Blanca, President of the Supreme Junta of the kingdom, Dean of his Majesty's Council of State, knight of the most noble order of the Golden Fleece, and Grand Cross of the Royal and illustrious order of Charles III, & c. Soon after the removal from Junta to Seville, death snatched him hence. *Seville Gazette*. *The True Republican or American Whig* [Vol. 1. No. 18] Wilmington, NC, Tuesday, 2 May 1809, page 4, column 2.

187. *Moldy Corn destructive to HORSES*. Colonel **Ward**, of Newark, New Jersey, within a few days has had fifteen very elegant horses to die, owing to their being fed on moldy corn; he calculates his loss at about 2000 dollars. A horse owned by Colonel **Ogden**, of the same place, also died after eating some of the same food. We make mention of this, that owners of horses may be careful to avoid giving them at any time corn that may be in the least moldy. *N. Jersey paper*. *The True Republican or American Whig* [Vol. 1. No. 18] Wilmington, NC, Tuesday, 2 May 1809, page 4, column 3.

188. TEN CENTS REWARD. ABSCONDED from the subscriber, an Apprentice to the Tailoring business, named *Dugald Valentine*. He is between 18 and 19 years of age. Whoever will apprehend and return him to the subscriber in Wilmington, shall receive the above reward, but no expenses will be paid. **D. M'KAY**. April 24. 3t. *The True Republican or American Whig* [Vol. 1. No. 18] Wilmington, NC, Tuesday, 2 May 1809, page 4, column 3. *The True Republican or American Whig* [Vol. 1. No. 20] Wilmington, NC, Tuesday, 16 May 1809, page 4, column 4. *The True Republican or American Whig* [Vol. 1. No. 21] Wilmington, NC, Tuesday, 23 May 1809, page 2, column 2.

189. HARMONIC SOCIETY. AT a meeting of the *Harmonic Society*, held on Saturday noon, the 22d instant. RESOLVED. That in consequence of the performance advertised for this evening for

the benefit of the Academy, our next regular meeting be postponed til Wednesday evening, the 26th inst. RESOLVED, That tickets of admission be issued for each ensuing regular meeting of this Society, at half a dollar each; the amount of which, after the necessary expenses of the evening are deducted, to be paid to the Trustees of the Academy, for the benefit of that institution. **J. FLEMING**, Sec. April 24. *The True Republican or American Whig* [Vol. 1. No. 18] Wilmington, NC, Tuesday, 2 May 1809, page 4, column 3.

190. ENCYCLOPEDIA PERTHENSIS, for sale at this office -- Price, elegant bound set, 80 dollars -- in boards, 60 dolls. *The True Republican or American Whig* [Vol. 1. No. 18] Wilmington, NC, Tuesday, 2 May 1809, page 4, column 3.

191. Cadiz February 23. PROCLAMATION. Our Lord the king Don **Ferdinand VII**,[30] and in his royal name, Don **Felix Jones**, field marshal of the royal armies, and governor pro tempore of this place, & c. In consequence of the discontents and commotions which have taken place in this city, whose inhabitants have requested various things which they consider useful and necessary to their private and public security, and to the exercise of their liberty and of the national independence, and considering their loyalty and patronage at all times, and particularly at present as also the signal and important services which they have performed and are now performing in favor of just cause which they defend at the hazard of their lives and fortunes, it is made known as follows: . . And that this may be known to and satisfy the public, and that the confidence due to the authorities may be restored, and all disturbances cease, and tranquility reign, without which the laws cannot govern, it is ordered that these presents be posted up in Cadiz, this 23d Feb. 1809. FR. **MARINO DE SEVILLA**, Guardian of Capuchins. **Felix Jones**. *The True Republican or American Whig* [Vol. 1. No. 19] Wilmington, NC, Tuesday, 9 May 1809, page 1, column 4 & page 2, column 1.

192. United States of America, State of North Carolina, District of Cape Fear, In Admiralty,} WHEREAS **Robert Hill Jones**, Esq. Attorney for the United States, for the District aforesaid, hath filed his Libel in the honorable court, setting forth that **Robert Cochrane**, Esq. Collector for the Port of Wilmington, in the District aforesaid, has seized as forfeited to the U. States, a certain Ship, called the MARY, and her Cargo, found on board, for the following cause, to wit; "That the said Ship hath received on board at her cargo, in the River Cape Fear, within the District aforesaid, 40 Bales of Cotton, 75 Tierces Casks of Flax Seed, and that the same or the greatest part thereof, were put on board said Ship since the 9th of January last past & that **John Clarke**, Junior, was the owner of the said Ship, at the time such articles and produce were put on board; and further, that the said **John Clarke**, junior, did put, place and load said articles on board his

---

[30] **Ferdinand VII** (1784–1833), king of Spain 1808–1833, son of **Charles IV** and **María Luisa**. Excluded from a role in the government, he became the center of intrigues against the chief minister **Manuel de Godoy** and attempted to win the support of Napoleon I. In 1807 he was arrested by his father, who accused him of plotting his overthrow and the murder of his mother and Godoy. He was soon forgiven, but the prestige of the family was shaken, and this facilitated Napoleon's invasion of Spain. A palace revolution at Aranjuez (March 1808) caused the dismissal of Godoy and the abdication of Charles in favor of Ferdinand, who was enthusiastically acclaimed by the people. Ferdinand was soon persuaded to cross the French border and meet Napoleon at Bayonne. There he was forced to renounce his throne in favor of Charles IV, who in turn resigned his rights to Napoleon. The emperor gave the Spanish throne to Joseph Bonaparte. During the Peninsular War (1808–14) Ferdinand was imprisoned in France. In his name the nationalist and liberal elements of Spain resisted the French invaders, and a liberal constitution was proclaimed (1812) by the Cortes at Cádiz. Throughout the Spanish Empire his name was the rallying cry of revolutionary elements. When Ferdinand was restored (1814) to his throne, however, he promptly abolished the liberal constitution and revealed himself a thorough reactionary. *The Columbia Encyclopedia, Sixth Edition* (Columbia University Press: 2001).

ship, with an intent to export transport and convey the same without the U. States to some foreign place; Kingdom, or Country, contrary to an act of Congress in such cases made and provided; and further, that the said **John Clarke**, junior, was aiding and abetting such illegal shipment and loading." And whereas the said **Robert Hill Jones** Attorney as aforesaid, doth pray, that the said ship Mary, her tackle, furniture, and apparel, and also the Cotton, Rice and Flax Seed, may be a decree of this honorable court, be declared forfeited to the United States: And whereas his honor, **Henry Potter** Esq. Judge of said court, has appointed the first Monday in June, to hear and determine said libel, at the Court-House in Wilmington; therefore all persons claiming the said Ship, her cargo, & c. are hereby notified to appear at the time & place aforesaid, and show cause, if any they can, why the said ship, her tackle, apparel, cargo & c. should not be Condemned to the use of the United Stats. Witness, **CARLETON WALKER**, *Clerk* Of Said Court at Wilmington. May 8, 1809. *The True Republican or American Whig* [Vol. 1. No. 19] Wilmington, NC, Tuesday, 9 May 1809, page 2, column 1.

193. AT A MEETING of the Commissioners of the town of Wilmington, On the 4th May, 1809. WHEREAS complaint hath been made to the Commissioners of the Town that the Baking business is carried on by slaves not authorized to carry on the same and that the Ovens are not constructed according to the Ordinance in that case made and provided: ORDERED That the said Ordinance be published in the Wilmington newspapers, and that the Town Constables be ordered & required to make enquiry, and if possible, to find out the persons offending as aforementioned, and report their names at the next meeting of the Commissioners,

ORDINANCE, THE Ovens to the Bake Houses in this Town shall be constructed after the following manner, viz: The Oven having been built in the ordinary way, a perpendicular wall shall then be erected around what is called the crown of said Oven, so as to be two feet above the same, and the space contained within said wall, shall be completely filled up with earth or sand; the floor of the apartment, or room, in a Bake house, immediately connected with or attached to the mouth or face of the Oven, shall be so constructed as to be rendered secure as possible, against the accident of taking fire from the oven. Every person who shall erect an oven in any House or tenement in this Town, for the purpose of Baking and vending Bread, *shall* before putting the same to use apply to the Commissioners of the town, to have the same inspected, and if on examination it shall be found to answer to all the above requisites, he shall be entitled to, and receive a Certificate from the Magistrate of Police, and thenceforth be allowed to carry on the Baking business in the same. Any person who shall be convicted of having erected an Oven for the purpose of Baking Bread for sale, and of putting the same to use without having first obtained a Certificate from the Magistrate of Police, as above prescribed, shall be subject to a penalty of fifty pounds. By order of the Commissioners, **THOS. CALLENDER**, T. Clerk. *The True Republican or American Whig* [Vol. 1. No. 19] Wilmington, NC, Tuesday, 9 May 1809, page 2, column 1.

194. NOTICE. WILL be put up at PUBLIC AUCTION to the lowest Bidder, at the School-House in Smithville, On Thursday the 15th day of June, at the hour of 1 o'clock, the building of a Court-house, Prison and Stocks, in that town, in the County of Brunswick, at which time and place, plans thereof will be produced and terms made known. Smithville, May 8. 3w. *The True Republican or American Whig* [Vol. 1. No. 19] Wilmington, NC, Tuesday, 9 May 1809, page 2, column 1. *The True Republican or American Whig* [Vol. 1. No. 20] Wilmington, NC, Tuesday, 16 May 1809, page 3, column 1. *The True Republican or American Whig* [Vol. 1. No. 21] Wilmington, NC, Tuesday, 23 May 1809, page 3, column 2. CONTRACT, Will be put up . . . By order of the Commissioners **JOHN CONYERS**, *Clerk.* Smithville, 29th April, 1809. *The Wilmington Gazette* [Number 646. 13th Year] Wilmington, NC, Tuesday, 23 May 1809, page 1, column 2.

195. *Scentium, vigiiiie, audoribusque, culligite, . .* From the knowledge I have of the French language, I have discovered that Boyer and Defetanville, have each of them omitted in their Dictionaries about five thousand French words, have inserted many badly spelt and many they have left undecided. I have put all in good order, and sent them to London. . . Verite quæso, domini, et inspicite scripti mea, et cum vultus vestri affulgebunt mim, gravior ibit dies. I had

lately chosen New-York for my residence, but the last winter has been so hard there, and I have suffered so much from the cold, that I resolved to go to a southern state, and have come to this place, although I had at New-York many scholars. . . I have concluded to teach young ladies and gentlemen of this place, the French language, & am sure they will make satisfactory progress, if their zeal answers to the cares I will have for them. Apply to me, at Mr. **Jesse Jennett**'s, in Orange Street. **DE CHANLA**. May 8. 2w. *The True Republican or American Whig* [Vol. 1. No. 19] Wilmington, NC, Tuesday, 9 May 1809, page 3, column 2.

196. JUST RECEIVED From Philadelphia, and for sale under the directions of **Robert W. Brown**, 4 tons Iron -- flat and square bars, 2 hhds, Whiskey, . . I doz. Chairs. May 8. 3w. *The True Republican or American Whig* [Vol. 1. No. 19] Wilmington, NC, Tuesday, 9 May 1809, page 3, column 2. *The True Republican or American Whig* [Vol. 1. No. 20] Wilmington, NC, Tuesday, 16 May 1809, page 3, column 1. *The True Republican or American Whig* [Vol. 1. No. 21] Wilmington, NC, Tuesday, 23 May 1809, page 4, column 4. *The Wilmington Gazette* [Number 646. 13th Year] Wilmington, NC, Tuesday, 23 May 1809, page 1, column 1.

197. WILMINGTON, February, Mar. 9, 1809. The Editors of this paper having a few days since, received a supply of new type from Philadelphia, they will be enabled to publish it in a larger form, as soon as paper of the proper size can be procured. *The True Republican or American Whig* [Vol. 1. No. 19] Wilmington, NC, Tuesday, 9 May 1809, page 3, column 2.

198. A Capt. Of a vessel direct from Charleston, has favored us with the following article. On Wednesday the 3d inst. At 6 P.M. the U. States Brig Hornet, arrived at Rebellion Roads, Charleston. In 20 minutes after, she was passed and saluted by a British sloop of war, that proceeded direct to Charleston, supposed to have dispatches on board. *The True Republican or American Whig* [Vol. 1. No. 19] Wilmington, NC, Tuesday, 9 May 1809, page 3, column 2.

199. A letter from Havana, dated April 10 received at New-York, says, "The French residents in the island are obliged to keep close on board of vessels, & c. on account of the rage of the populace. American vessels that have arrived are overhauled by the Spanish officers, to ascertain if they have any French property on board. Money is very scarce. Sugar from 4 to 6 dollars, coffee 16. So sale for any articles." *The True Republican or American Whig* [Vol. 1. No. 19] Wilmington, NC, Tuesday, 9 May 1809, page 3, column 4.

200. The British packet Carteret, **Patterson**, arrived at New York on the 23d ult from Falmouth, which place she left the 25th of March. London papers to the 9th of March were received. One of the papers of that date states that the accounts from Spain are of a very gratifying nature. . . Saragossa not only held out with unabated firmness, but had obtained great advantages over the French. The women of that place, it seems, had by an ingenious device, been chiefly instrumental in obtaining these advantages, having appeared before the wall as desperate with distress, and inviting the enemy to put an end to their suffering by a decisive attack on the town. A large body of the French, on the 17th January was induced, by this stratagem, to pour into the town, where the patriots were ready to receive them, and destroyed a great number. Many of those intrepid females fell in the conflict. It is said **Cuesta** and the Duke **Del Infantado** had united their forces, and were marching for Toledo with 60,000 men. *The True Republican or American Whig* [Vol. 1. No. 19] Wilmington, NC, Tuesday, 9 May 1809, page 3, column 4.

201. Dispatches from Admiral **Stopford**, and letters from officers in his fleet, speak confidently of the destruction or capture of most of the Brest fleet now at Rochefort. Three frigates have been much shattered and drove aground. The British continued to receive supplies from the United States, as will be seen by our ship news department. In addition to the list of vessels expected from England there are twenty ships & brigs loading at Liverpool for British America. Those taking freight to the U. States, engage to "land the goods in Canada and Nova Scotia if our ports shall have been shut against British manufacturers." Very great quantities of merchandise may be

expected. *The True Republican or American Whig* [Vol. 1. No. 19] Wilmington, NC, Tuesday, 9 May 1809, page 3, column 4.

202. Marine List. Port of Wilmington. ENTERED. Sch'r Venus, **Wadham**, New-York. Sch'r Sea Horse, **Wheaton**, Charleston. Sch'r Maria, **Griffin**, Charleston. Sloop Morning Star, **Owens**, Philadelphia. Sch'r Enterprize, **Backius**, Philadelphia. Sch'r Regulator, **M'Ilhenny**, Charleston. Sch'r Betsy, **Holmes**, Plymouth, N.C. Swedish Sch'r Isabella, **Barkham**, Malanzas, cargo, Sugar & Coffee, to **H. Kelly**. Sch'r Catharine, **Jones**, Charleston. CLEARED. Ship Charles Carter, **Drysdale**, N. York. Sch'r Traveller, **Rich**, Boston. Sch'r Gulielma, **Montgomery**, Charleston. Brig Catharine, **Curtis**, Philadelphia. Sloop Morning Star, **Owens**, Philadelphia. Sch'r Comet, **Jenkins**, New-York. Sch'r Maria, **Griffin**, Philadelphia. *The True Republican or American Whig* [Vol. 1. No. 19] Wilmington, NC, Tuesday, 9 May 1809, page 3, column 4.

203. BENGAL. The kingdom of Bengal, in the happy times of the Mogul government is described as exhibiting the most charming and picturesque scenery. Opening into extensive glades covered with a fine turf & interspersed with woods filled with a variety of birds of beautiful colors: amongst others, peacocks in abundance sitting on the vast horizontal branches, displayed their dazzling plumes to the sun: the Ganges winding its mighty waters through the adjacent plains added to the prospect inexpressible grandeur: whilst the artist at his loom, under the immense shades of the banyan tree, softened his labor by the tender strains of music. *The True Republican or American Whig* [Vol. 1. No. 19] Wilmington, NC, Tuesday, 9 May 1809, page 4, column 4.

204. Burgos, (Spain), March 5. Gen. **Sebastiani** pursues his success. Marshals **Junot** and **St. Seyr**, are approaching Valencia, which it is expected will not make any defense. Saragossa surrendered the 19th Feb. to the duke of Montebello, (Lasnes). Such of the garrison as would not swear allegiance to Joseph I. were to be sent prisoners of war into France. *The True Republican or American Whig* [Vol. 1. No. 20] Wilmington, NC, Tuesday, 16 May 1809, page 2, column 2.

205. March 5. A vast number of officers, subjects of the Princes of the Rhinnish confederacy, have positively refused to bear arms against their countrymen. The departure of the French Ambassador has occasioned a very lively sensation at this place. *The True Republican or American Whig* [Vol. 1. No. 20] Wilmington, NC, Tuesday, 16 May 1809, page 2, column 3.

206. Many means offer for penetrating into Insurgent Ireland, and for seeking the remains of Sir **John Moore**'s army in the country of Kent. -- When Carthage carried her arms into Italy, the Romans soon found themselves under her own walls in Africa, and the *rival of Rome disappeared!!! The True Republican or American Whig* [Vol. 1. No. 20] Wilmington, NC, Tuesday, 16 May 1809, page 2, column 3.

207. An epidemic disease was said in the French papers, to have broken out at Saragossa, in consequence of the suffering and hardships endured in the siege, and to have carried off upwards of twenty thousand persons. *The True Republican or American Whig* [Vol. 1. No. 20] Wilmington, NC, Tuesday, 16 May 1809, page 2, column 3.

208. Council of Prizes, Paris, Jan. 25. The American vessel Susan, has been adjudged good prize to the officers and crews of the Italian and Cyrene frigates. The same court has declared good and lawful prize the merchandize taken out of the American ship Augusta, by the French privateer L'Eve, and confiscated the same for the benefit of the Marine Invalid Case. *The True Republican or American Whig* [Vol. 1. No. 20] Wilmington, NC, Tuesday, 16 May 1809, page 2, column 3.

209. London, March 3. *Commercial Treaty with New Portugal.* The commercial treaty which is now carrying on between our Ambassador as the Brazilian court & the government of that country is, we understand, founded on a basis that is likely to contribute equally to the interest of both parties. In the mean time, a new tariff has been established at Rio Janeiro, which

considerably reduces the valuation at which British goods had previously been rated, and which is, consequently, tantamount to a diminution of the import duties, as they are charged *ad valorem*. A new warehousing system is said to have been also in contemplation when the last accounts came away, and that it was to be framed upon a principle similar to our own. *The True Republican or American Whig* [Vol. 1. No. 20] Wilmington, NC, Tuesday, 16 May 1809, page 2, columns 3 & 4.

210. *For the True Republican*. What can be urged against the embargo? Nothing certainly. It has produced the effects which were contemplated at its adoption. It was intended, 1. As a measure to call home our property and seamen which were on the high seas, And 2. To coerce Great Britain to rescind her orders. . . If, however, the Federalists will contend that the Non-intercourse act, and not the embargo, has effected this change, let them have it so both are Republican measures -- both were opposed to them, and attach the credit to which they please, the honor is due to the REPUBLICANS, and to them only. MENTOR. *The True Republican or American Whig* [Vol. 1. No. 20] Wilmington, NC, Tuesday, 16 May 1809, page 2, column 4 & page 3, column 1.

211. REGIMENTAL ORDERS. THE Officers commanding companies in the first or lower battalion of New Hanover County Militia, are required to appear with their respective companies, armed and equipped, agreeably to law, on the usual parade ground in Wilmington, on Saturday the 27th inst. In order for inspection and filling up the detachment of 36 men, being the additional quota of the corps as provided by law. The commissioned Officers are further required to appear at the court-house in Wilmington, completely armed and equipped, on the day immediately preceding the above, with rolls of their companies, compleat. The Calvary and Artillery companies will parade with the Battalion. By order of the Col. Command't, **SAM'L BLUDWORTH**, 1ST Major of N. Hanover Reg't. May 12. *The True Republican or American Whig* [Vol. 1. No. 20] Wilmington, NC, Tuesday, 16 May 1809, page 3, column 2. *The Wilmington Gazette* [Number 646. 13th Year] Wilmington, NC, Tuesday, 23 May 1809, page 1, column 1.

212. *FRENCH LANGUAGE*. To convince the gentlemen of letters that Boyer has left a great many words undecided, I here add some. Acense ou acensement, adonion ou adonique, . . I will receive a few scholars more, and if at the end of the first month, the parents, & c. are not satisfied with my method of teaching, I will ask nothing for my trouble, except two dollars which shall have been paid; . . Apply to me, at Mr. **Jesse Jennett**'s, in Orange-street. **DE CHANLA**. Any person who may wish to purchase a good English hunting GUN will please to apply as above. May 13. *The True Republican or American Whig* [Vol. 1. No. 20] Wilmington, NC, Tuesday, 16 May 1809, page 3, column 2. *The True Republican or American Whig* [Vol. 1. No. 21] Wilmington, NC, Tuesday, 23 May 1809, page 4, column 4.

213. *RUNAWAY NEGRO*. A reward of FIFTY DOLLARS will be given to any person who will apprehend and bring to the subscriber, or confine in any jail within the state so that I get him, a certain Negro Man by the name of **JOHN**. He is about forty years of age, upwards of 6 feet high, speaks broken English, and is considerably ruptured, which may be plainly perceived. He was born and raised in the island of St. Croix; is a tolerable good sailor, and I expect he will endeavor to get on board of a vessel, by calling himself a free man. It is probable he is lurking about Wilmington or Newbern, or in the neighborhood of Mr. **Edward Hatch**, Jun. on Trent River, in Jones County, as he has a wife there. All captains of vessels, or other persons, are forewarned from concealing or harboring of the said Negro, under the penalty of the law. **EDWARD WARD**, Jun. Onslow County, May 10. tf. *The True Republican or American Whig* [Vol. 1. No. 20] Wilmington, NC, Tuesday, 16 May 1809, page 3, column 2. *The True Republican or American Whig* [Vol. 1. No. 21] Wilmington, NC, Tuesday, 23 May 1809, page 4, column 3. *The True Republican or American Whig* [Vol. 1. No. 23] Wilmington, NC, Tuesday, 6 June 1809, page 1, column 1. *The True Republican or American Whig* [Vol. 1. No. 25] Wilmington, NC, Tuesday, 20 June 1809, page 4, column 3. *The True Republican or American Whig* [Vol. 1. No. 27] Wilmington, NC, Tuesday, 4 July 1809, page 4, column 3.

214. VALUABLE LAND FOR SALE. TWO hundred Acres, situated on the North-East River, about six miles below South Washington, and adjoining the lands of **James Smith** and **Thomas Bludworth**; the soil of which is equal, if not superior, to any in the neighborhood. As no person will purchase without first viewing the land, it is necessary here to give a further description of it. Any person wishing to purchase, can be accommodated by applying to the subscriber in Wilmington. **LEWIS BLUDWORTH**. May 16. tf. *The True Republican or American Whig* [Vol. 1. No. 20] Wilmington, NC, Tuesday, 16 May 1809, page 2, column 3. *The True Republican or American Whig* [Vol. 1. No. 21] Wilmington, NC, Tuesday, 23 May 1809, page 4, column 3. *The True Republican or American Whig* [Vol. 1. No. 23] Wilmington, NC, Tuesday, 6 June 1809, page 1, column 1. *The True Republican or American Whig* [Vol. 1. No. 25] Wilmington, NC, Tuesday, 20 June 1809, page 4, column 4.

215. TWENTY DOLLARS REWARD. RUNAWAY from the subscriber about the 20th of April last, an Apprentice boy, about 18 years of age, named **THOMAS BELL**. I will give the above reward to any person who will deliver the said boy to me in Wilmington. **BENJAMIN JACOB**. May 14. *The True Republican or American Whig* [Vol. 1. No. 20] Wilmington, NC, Tuesday, 16 May 1809, page 2, column 3. *The True Republican or American Whig* [Vol. 1. No. 21] Wilmington, NC, Tuesday, 23 May 1809, page 2, column 2. *The True Republican or American Whig* [Vol. 1. No. 25] Wilmington, NC, Tuesday, 20 June 1809, page 1, column 1. *The True Republican or American Whig* [Vol. 1. No. 27] Wilmington, NC, Tuesday, 4 July 1809, page 4, column 3.

216. ALL ACCOUNTS. Against GUN-BOATS, No. 7 and 166, will please be handed in at the counting room of **T. N. GAUTIER**. May 15. *The True Republican or American Whig* [Vol. 1. No. 20] Wilmington, NC, Tuesday, 16 May 1809, page 3, column 2. *The Wilmington Gazette* [Number 646. 13th Year] Wilmington, NC, Tuesday, 23 May 1809, page 2, column 1. *The True Republican or American Whig* [Vol. 1. No. 25] Wilmington, NC, Tuesday, 20 June 1809, page 4, column 1.

217. The Federal Court for the North Carolina district, commenced at Raleigh on the 12th instant. *The True Republican or American Whig* [Vol. 1. No. 20] Wilmington, NC, Tuesday, 16 May 1809, page 2, column 3.

218. We learn by the sch'r Richard Captain **Bradford**, in twelve days from Havana that the riotous proceedings in that place, had in a great measure, subsided. The French inhabitants however by permission, were selling their property to the best possible advantages, and hurrying off. *The True Republican or American Whig* [Vol. 1. No. 20] Wilmington, NC, Tuesday, 16 May 1809, page 3, columns 3 & 4.

219. This morning (says a Louisville paper of April 12) Mr. **Benjamin Wilkinson** with a hardy band of warriors, hunters & trappers, all well armed and equipped, for a three years expedition, left this place for St. Louis: there to join the St. Louis Missouri Company, who intend to push their trade to the River Columbia, and probably in a few years, by that route, to the East Indies.. *The True Republican or American Whig* [Vol. 1. No. 20] Wilmington, NC, Tuesday, 16 May 1809, page 3, column 4. *From the National Intelligence.* GENTLEMEN, I was pleased at observing your paper of the 3d inst. under the Louisburg head that. . . He is the son of General **Joseph Wilkinson** of Maryland, and received his commercial knowledge principally from Gen. **John Mason** of Georgetown, with whom he lived for five or six years. . . AMICUS. *Washington City, May* 6, 1809. *The True Republican or American Whig* [Vol. 1. No. 21] Wilmington, NC, Tuesday, 23 May 1809, page 2, column 3.

220. The Halifax papers contain a splendid account of the arrival of Sir **George Prevost** at that place, with his gallant troops, whose bravery in the reduction of Martinique prepared them a cordial and grateful welcome. *The True Republican or American Whig* [Vol. 1. No. 20] Wilmington, NC, Tuesday, 16 May 1809, page 3, column 4.

221. CHINA -- Letters from Paris state, that the emperor of China, his family, & the principal Mandarins have become converts to the Roman Catholic [faith] Religion. Political changes are expected in that great empire, under the tuition of French agents. *The True Republican or American Whig* [Vol. 1. No. 20] Wilmington, NC, Tuesday, 16 May 1809, page 3, column 4.

222. Messrs. Editors; There has a report circulated for some time in this place, injuries to the character of Lieut. **Stephen B**. **Daniel**, of the U. States 3d Regiment of Infantry; of which it is said, that I am the principal cause. To clear to the world the character of a man who so unjustly suffers, I think proper here to state the circumstances which happened between Lieut. **Daniel** and myself. Sometime in February last, when Lieut. **D**. was in this place recruiting, we happened to board at the same tavern, and were intimate. One evening after Lieut. **D**. had lain down, I went into the chamber where he was, when we fell into conversation. I was going to take a seat in a chair that stood by the bed, he observed that his coat was in the chair, and that I might probably injure his epaulet; when I ignorantly and inoffensively unbuttoned it from his coat. After he had perceived the joke, (for nothing more did I intend it) he was angry; and, as I understood, had thrown out some threats. When I heard this, I immediately went to see him, and directly perceived his resentment, when I repeatedly declared to him the purity of my intention, and made all acknowledgements which I thought necessary' and which no gentleman could refuse. Because Lieut. **Daniel** did not give way to an impulse of passion, and sacrifice my life, some persons have laid hold of the opportunity to speak ill of his character, and have added greatly to the report by saying, that I cut his epaulet off his shoulder, and that he treated me with half a dozen of wine for a restoration of it. All of which I do declare to the world to be malicious falsehoods. I have taken this method, sirs, of making known to the public the circumstance just as it happened, and also the purity of my intention -- that is, I positively did not mean any insult to Lieut. **Daniel**, nor intend any [the newspaper is damaged here]. **JOHN BARKMAN**. Wilmington, May 10.

N. B. The Lieutenant having called for a bottle of wine some time after he told me my acknowledgments were satisfactory was polite enough to ask me to take a glass, from which it must have been inferred that he treated me. I also declare that I did not receive or consider it as a treat for the return of his epaulet. **J. B.**

It is to be remembered that Capt. **J. Barkman** [Swedish Sch'r Isabella] sailed a few days after the above mentioned circumstances happened, and has just returned. *The True Republican or American Whig* [Vol. 1. No. 20] Wilmington, NC, Tuesday, 16 May 1809, page 3, column 4.

223. *MARRIED* -- At Newbern, on the 4th inst. **Thomas Watson**, Editor of the Herald, and one of the proprietors of this paper, to Miss **Sarah Graves Hannis**, both of that place.[31] *The True Republican or American Whig* [Vol. 1. No. 20] Wilmington, NC, Tuesday, 16 May 1809, page 3, column 4.

---

[31] When planning to marry, the prospective groom took out a bond from the clerk of the court in the county where the bride had her usual residence as surety that there was no legal obstacle to the proposed marriage. Most of the bonds contain the following information: groom's name, bride's name, date of bond, bondsmen, and witnesses. **Thomas Watson** and **Sarah Graves Hannis** had a bond recorded in Craven County on 4 May 1809, Book 3 page 361. The bondsman was **John R. Donnell** and the witness was **J. G. Stanly**. **Sarah Hannis**, also called Sally, was the daughter of **Elizabeth Hannis**, and they are mentioned in the will of her maternal aunt **Mary Crispin**, 22 April 1805, Craven County. Mrs. Watson died at the age of 73 in St. Louis, Missouri, 31 August 1863 and her remains were buried in Bellefontaine Cemetery. **Thomas Watson** lived to the age of 84 and died in St. Louis, 7 April 1870. 1809 was also a year of sadness for Thomas Watson. His brother **James Watson** committed suicide in August in Wilmington and unfortunately his other brother, Ensign **Robert Watson** died in October while marching from New Orleans to Natchez. *St. Louis City Death Records, 1850-1908*, Volume K, page 190 and Volume 3, page 238. Appreciation to Jo Ann E. Murphy and Eual P. Beauchamp for *Marriages of Craven County 1851-1908 & Marriage Bonds 1773-1869*, and to Stephen E. Bradley, *Craven County, North Carolina, Volume 3, 1801-1812, (Wills)*, and also thanks to Lois S. Neal, *Abstracts of Vital Records from Raleigh, North Carolina Newspapers 1799-1819* (1979).

224. Marine List. PORT OF WILMINGTON. ENTERED. Sch'r Betsy, **Wilson**, New-River. Brig Equator, **Ingersoll**, Boston. Sloop George, **Bowen**, Providence R.I. Sch'r Anubah & Ruthy, **White**, Newport. Sch'r Mercury, **Ireson**, Charleston. Sch'r Clairs & Eliza, **Kennedy**, Charleston. Brig Sally, **Cameron**, Charleston. Brig Matilda, **Brown**, Charleston. CLEARED. Sch'r Resolution, **Bates**, Beston. Ship Perserverance, **Bowman**, New-York. Sch'r Milly, **Rhodes**, Charleston. Sch'r Temperance, **Wellman**, Boston. Sch'r Rebecca, **Smith**, Boston. Sch'r Betsey, **Wilson**, New-River. Sch'r Venus, **Wadham**, New-York. Sch'r Sea Horse, **Wheaton**, Philad. Brig Nancy, **Davis**, Boston. Sch'r Betsy, **Holmes**, New-York. *The True Republican or American Whig* [Vol. 1. No. 20] Wilmington, NC, Tuesday, 16 May 1809, page 3, column 4.

225. Communication From the late President **Adams**. THE INADMISSIBLE PRINICPLES of the King of England's Proclamation of Oct. 22, 1807 -- Considered. . . Quincy, January 9, 1809. Sir -- In my letter of the 25th of Dec., it was remarked, that the proclamation from pressing seamen from our merchant ships had not been sufficiently reprobated. . . (*To be continued.*) *The True Republican or American Whig* [Vol. 1. No. 20] Wilmington, NC, Tuesday, 16 May 1809, page 4, columns 1 - 3. That the practice of impressments of seamen was legal . . . *The True Republican or American Whig* [Vol. 1. No. 21] Wilmington, NC, Tuesday, 23 May 1809, page 1, columns 1 - 4. To the editors of the Boston Patriot. SIRS -- A few words more on the subject of pressing. . . **JOHN ADAMS**. Quincy, April 25, 1809. *The True Republican or American Whig* [Vol. 1. No. 23] Wilmington, NC, Tuesday, 6 June 1809, page 2, columns 1 - 2.

226. AGRICULTURAL. *The method recommended as follows, is by one of the first planters in South-Carolina.* Begin to plant about the 25th of March, trench shallow and wide, and scatter the seed in the row; make 72 or 75 rows in a task, and sow two bushels to an acre.

1st. Hoe about the end of April or beginning of May, when the rice is in the fourth leaf; then flood and clear the field of trash. If planting be late, and you are likely to be in grass, flood before hoeing; but hoeing first is preferable. The best depth to flood is three or four inches. It is a good mark to see the tops of the rice just out of the water; the deep places are not to be regarded, the rice will grow through in 3 or 4 days. Observe to make a notch on the frame of the trunk, when the water is at a proper depth: if the rains rise the water above the notch or it leaks out, add, or let off accordingly. This is done by putting a small stick in the door of the trunk, about an inch in diameter; if scum or froth appear in eight or ten days, freshen the water, take off the trunk door, run off the water with one ebb, and take in the next *flood*: then regulate as before. Keep the water on about fifteen or seventeen days, counting from the day the field is flooded; then leak off with a small stick for two days, then run off the whole, and keep the field dry. In four or five days after, hoe the second time, stir the ground whether clean or not, and comb up the fallen rice with the fingers. Keep dry and hoe through the field. Hoe the third time and pick clean. Then flood as you hoe. Let the water be the same depth as before. If any grass has escaped, it must be picked in the water after it shoots out. This is called the fourth hoeing, but the hoe is never used, except for some high places or to clean the dams. If the rice is flaggy and likely to lodge, flood deep to support it, and keep it on until the harvest. *The True Republican or American Whig* [Vol. 1. No. 20] Wilmington, NC, Tuesday, 16 May 1809, page 4, column 3.

227. ANECDOTES. A gentleman having a pad that started and broke his wife's neck, a neighboring squire told him he wished to purchase him for his wife to ride upon, "No," says the other, "I shall not sell the little fellow, because I intend to marry again myself." *The True Republican or American Whig* [Vol. 1. No. 20] Wilmington, NC, Tuesday, 16 May 1809, page 4, column 4.

228. Supplementary DIVISION ORDERS. IT having been represented that such delays may probably arise from the state of the Roads and Ferries, as to render more time necessary for arrival at some of the Counties than has been allowed in the Division Orders of the 30th March; the following alterations have been adopted, of which the proper officers will take and give due

notice. The Review in Craven County on Saturday the 20th. In Carteret on Wednesday the 24th. In Onslow on Friday the 26th.} Of May next.

☞ THE Commanding Officers of Brunswick, New-Hanover, Pitt, Lenoir, Greene, Johnston and Wayne, will have their Regiments in readiness to be reviewed in the course of a few months. *Br order of Major General* **SMITH**. *JACOB LEONARD*, A.D.C. Belvedere, April 21, 1809. 2w. The True Republican or American Whig [Vol. 1. No. 20] Wilmington, NC, Tuesday, 16 May 1809, page 4, column 4.

229. *From the Boston Chronicle*. It is mortifying to observe how far the British factions in America have been able to deceive the citizens in the northern states, with respect to the conduct of the federal administration. . . The True Republican or American Whig [Vol. 1. No. 21] Wilmington, NC, Tuesday, 23 May 1809, page 2, columns 1 -2.

230. *Marietta May* 1. The eastern mail, which arrived on Wednesday, brought the pleasing intelligence of the happy adjustment of our controversies with Great Britain.

On this important and joyful occasion, the citizens of the town of Marietta [Ohio] assembled in the evening on the commons near the market-house, elevated the cannon on a commanding eminence, and broke the silence of night with her seventeen thunders, accompanied by the ringing of the bell and shouts of citizens. Men of both political parties were present. . . A great number of volunteer toasts were drunk on the occasion, amongst which were the following: *America, Commerce and Freedom* . . . *The occasion* . . . *The Western Wilderness* -- Its fertile bosom the future nurse of nations. *Agriculture* -- Weep not damsel, thy sister commerce is delivered out of all her troubles. The True Republican or American Whig [Vol. 1. No. 21] Wilmington, NC, Tuesday, 23 May 1809, page 2, columns 2 - 3.

231. FOREIGN INTELLIGENCE. *London, March 21.* Accounts have been received to the 7th of March from the coast of Spain, near Vigo, Pontevedra, and Villa Gracias. That part of the country is in open and determined insurrection against the French. There have already been several skirmishes, and the peasants, we are happy to hear, have been often successful. . . The True Republican or American Whig [Vol. 1. No. 21] Wilmington, NC, Tuesday, 23 May 1809, page 2, column 3.

232. *Sweden*. -- We communicated yesterday the intelligence of an insurrection in Sweden. It is said that several thousand peasants have risen in the province of Weirmland[32], and were proceeding from Carlstadt to the capital. We have heard that a general officer put himself at the head of a body of military, and taken possession of Stockholm, whence the king had retired under the protection of about three thousand troops, who have remained faithful to his person. . . The True Republican or American Whig [Vol. 1. No. 21] Wilmington, NC, Tuesday, 23 May 1809, page 2, column 3. Sweden, it is said, is in a state of revolution and the report, though it cannot be absolutely relied on, is, that the insurgents have got possession of Stockholm, and put to death the king. The distressed situation of the country, arising from a protracted war, and the consequent heavy taxes, are stated to be the cause of the revolution. The Wilmington Gazette [Number 646. 13th Year] Wilmington, NC, Tuesday, 23 May 1809, page 3, column 2.

233. Being decisively of opinion, that France ought never to possess again a foot of land in the West Indies, we trust that ministers will take the earliest opportunity, after the capture of Martinique and Guadeloupe, to declare that she shall not: and to make known their determination never to give back those islands. The True Republican or American Whig [Vol. 1. No. 21] Wilmington, NC, Tuesday, 23 May 1809, page 2, column 4.

---

[32] Värmland is a historical province or *landskap* in the west of middle Sweden. It borders Västergötland, Dalsland, Dalarna, Västmanland and Närke. It is also bounded by Norway in the west. Its Latin name is *Wermelandia*; its English derivative is *Wermland* or similar variation. The origin of the name is uncertain. It may refer to a lake by that name, or to a river.

234. *Paris, March* 12. We are assured that his Imperial Majesty has bestowed the government general of the department of Tuscany on her imperial highness princess **Eliza**, sister of the emperor, and princess of Lucca and Plombino, with the title of grand duchess. Her husband, prince **Felix**, of Lucca and Plombino, is general of division, and commands the troops of Tuscany. By a decree of the 3d inst., the emperor has also created the eldest son of the king of Holland, **Napoleon Louis**, grand duke of Berg and Cleves. *The True Republican or American Whig* [Vol. 1. No. 21] Wilmington, NC, Tuesday, 23 May 1809, page 2, column 4.

235. *Lower Elbe, March* 6. According to intelligence from Sweden, the king had forbidden the introduction of English newspapers into his dominions, not on account of any hostile disposition towards England, but because some of the English newspapers express themselves in a style concerning Swedish affairs, which the king fears may produce unpleasant effects upon the minds of his subjects. *The True Republican or American Whig* [Vol. 1. No. 21] Wilmington, NC, Tuesday, 23 May 1809, page 2, column 4.

236. JUST ARRIVED. *And for sale by the subscriber*. A few half bls: Philadelphia superfine FLOUR. Half bls: ditto mess Beef. Phila. Ship & Pilot Bread of a superior quality. Irish Potatoes in Barrels. Kegs Philadelphia Butter. FCG, FG, FFG} Gun-Powder in Kegs. *T. N. GAUTIER.* May 22. tf. *The True Republican or American Whig* [Vol. 1. No. 21] Wilmington, NC, Tuesday, 23 May 1809, page 3, column 2. *The True Republican or American Whig* [Vol. 1. No. 23] Wilmington, NC, Tuesday, 6 June 1809, page 2, column 2. *The True Republican or American Whig* [Vol. 1. No. 25] Wilmington, NC, Tuesday, 20 June 1809, page 4, column 3. *The True Republican or American Whig* [Vol. 1. No. 27] Wilmington, NC, Tuesday, 4 July 1809, page 4, column 4.

237. *To the Freemen of New-Hanover County*. I beg leave to submit the following statement to facts. -- In July last, Mr. **William Hill**, who is now a candidate for a seat in the next General Assembly, purchased from me a quantity of refuse lumber -- I showed him the inspector's bill, and he send his workman to see the lumber, when he gave me his note for seventy-five dollars, payable about the 10th of October following. He said he wanted time, for he had rather be in h--- than asked for money. On the 18th instant, I spoke to him for the money -- He said he would leave it to men -- I told him if I left it to men, it should be to twelve men. We then parted. I went to a lawyer, and while he was filling up the writ, Mr. **Camack** told me that Mr. **Hill** wanted to see me. I went and met him, when he asked me what I had determined to do? I answered, that I had sued him. He said I was a d----d scoundrel, and that was my general character, and before I had time to make a reply, he knocked me down with a whip, and struck me several times after I was down. **P. HODGES**. Wilmington, May 21. *The True Republican or American Whig* [Vol. 1. No. 21] Wilmington, NC, Tuesday, 23 May 1809, page 3, column 2. *The True Republican or American Whig* [Vol. 1. No. 23] Wilmington, NC, Tuesday, 6 June 1809, page 4, column 3.

238. *THIRD AND LAST CALL!* **William Dick** give this positive, public and final notice, to those persons who are indebted to him, that unless they come forward and settle their accounts with him on or before the 20th of June next, such accounts shall be immediately put in suit. It is a step, he will take with reluctance, but, unless prevented by the mode suggested, it *must* be done. *May* 16. tf. *The True Republican or American Whig* [Vol. 1. No. 21] Wilmington, NC, Tuesday, 23 May 1809, page 3, column 2. *The Wilmington Gazette* [Number 646. 13th Year] Wilmington, NC, Tuesday, 23 May 1809, page 2, column 1. *The True Republican or American Whig* [Vol. 1. No. 23] Wilmington, NC, Tuesday, 6 June 1809, page 4, column 4. *The True Republican or American Whig* [Vol. 1. No. 25] Wilmington, NC, Tuesday, 20 June 1809, page 4, column 3.

239. One Hundred Cents reward. ABSCONDED from the Subscriber an Apprentice Boy named **LARKINS ROWE**, about 19 years of age, (as may be seen by his indentures.) All persons are forbid harboring or employing said Runaway. **JOHN MacCOLL**. May 23. *The True Republican or American Whig* [Vol. 1. No. 21] Wilmington, NC, Tuesday, 23 May 1809, page 3, column 2. *The Wilmington Gazette* [Number 646. 13th Year] Wilmington, NC, Tuesday, 23 May 1809, page 2, column 4.

240. The Federal Court was opened in this city on the 12th, says the *Raleigh Minerva*, by Chief Justice Marshall, and the District Judge Mr. [**Henry**] **Potter**.[33] On Monday last, the trial of **Allen Twitty** for counterfeiting Bank Bills came on. After a tedious examination of witnesses & lengthy arguments by Mr. **R. H. Jones**, Attorney for the United States, and Mr. **Gaston** for defendant, the latter took exceptions to a flaw in the bill of indictment; as it was not a literal copy of the Bank Bill upon which the indictment was founded; the word "demand" was omitted. The Court, therefore, directed the clerk to tear off the Bank Bill from the bill of indictment, as it could not go to the jury as evidence. The jury retired, and in a few minutes returned with a verdict of acquittal. **Twitty** was then remained to the custody of the Marshall, and was afterwards bound to appear at next term, to answer a charge upon the same bill. The indictment against **Twitty** had been hung up for some years. The late worthy attorney must have been much hurried, or his usual accuracy would have detected the omission in the bill of indictment. The trial of **Collins** was put off at his instance for the want of witnesses. *The True Republican or American Whig* [Vol. 1. No. 21] Wilmington, NC, Tuesday, 23 May 1809, page 3, column 3.

241. War Department, 29th April 1809. Sir -- I am directed by the President of the United States to inform your Excellency that the Detachment of Militia, made in pursuance of a communication to your Excellency from this department, bearing date the 29th day of October 1808, is no longer required to be held in readiness for actual service: . . . I have the honor to be, & c: **WILLIAM EUSTIS**, *Secretary for the Department of War*. *The True Republican or American Whig* [Vol. 1. No. 21] Wilmington, NC, Tuesday, 23 May 1809, page 3, column 3. We learn that a similar circular has been sent to the executive of North Carolina. *The Wilmington Gazette* [Number 646. 13th Year] Wilmington, NC, Tuesday, 23 May 1809, page 3, column 3.

242. His Excellency **Robert Wright**, Governor of Maryland, having resigned, the Legislature of that state are to meet on the 5th of June to appoint a successor. *The True Republican or American Whig* [Vol. 1. No. 21] Wilmington, NC, Tuesday, 23 May 1809, page 3, column 3. *The Wilmington Gazette* [Number 646. 13th Year] Wilmington, NC, Tuesday, 23 May 1809, page 2, column 4.

243. INDIAN WAR. Governor [**William Henry**] **Harrison** received on Monday last, a special express from Gov. **Lewis**, by which he is informed that an association has been entered into by a band of the Winnebagoes, and Puans, now living on the Illinois River, with others of the same nations, residing in Louisiana, and by the Iowas, and some other of the Mississippi tribes, for the purpose of attacking Fort Belle View (a fort lately erected by the United States on the Mississippi in the neighborhood of the De Moin) and waging war on the frontiers of Illinois and Louisiana. A party of the above association had made their appearance in the settlement of Goshen, in the county of St. Clair, a few days before the express set out, all armed with *new muskets*, and had taken off in their retreat with 15 horses. They were pursued by Capt. **Whitesides**, who, with his party had been cut off; the report, however, was not credited by the Governor. It gives us pleasure to say that were are authorized by Gov. **Harrison**, explicitly to state, that he has every reason to

---

[33] The Hon. **Henry Potter** was appointed Judge of the United States District Court in North Carolina on 7 April 1802. His district was Albemarle, Pamptico and Cape Fear. His date of separation was in 1809. Prior to his appointment he was the United States Circuit Judge. He was elected a Ruling Elder in the First Presbyterian Church in June 1826. Potter was born in 1765 and died on Sunday 20 December 1857 near Fayetteville, North Carolina. He was buried in Cross Creek Cemetery in Cumberland County, next to his spouse **Sylvia W. Potter** (1779-1853). John L. Cheney, *North Carolina Government 1585 - 1979, a Narrative and Statistical History* (Raleigh: North Carolina Department of the Secretary of State, 1981) page 753; *The Daily Journal* [Vol. 7, No. 91] Wilmington, NC, Tuesday Evening, 22 December 1857, page 2, column 1. Thanks to Helen Moore Sammons for abstracting the newspaper; Anna Sutton Sherman, *Cross Creek Cemetery Number One, Cumberland County, Fayetteville, North Carolina* (Katana Co., 1988) page 15.

believe that the tribes of the Wabash continue firm and unshaken in their attachment to the United States. *Vincennes paper* [Indiana]. *The True Republican or American Whig* [Vol. 1. No. 21] Wilmington, NC, Tuesday, 23 May 1809, page 3, column 4. From an express received by Gov. **Harrison** from Gov. **Lewis**, it appears that a few tribes of Indians on the Illinois River and residing in Louisiana have associated to wage war on our frontier settlements in those parts. *The Wilmington Gazette* [Number 646. 13th Year] Wilmington, NC, Tuesday, 23 May 1809, page 3, column 2.

244. MARRIED -- On Thursday evening last [18 May], at Cedar Grove, on the Sound, by the Rev. **Solomon Halling**, Mr. **Thomas Mabson**, to Miss **Elizabeth Moore**.[34] *The True Republican or American Whig* [Vol. 1. No. 21] Wilmington, NC, Tuesday, 23 May 1809, page 3, column 4. *COURT OF HYMEN*. *The Wilmington Gazette* [Number 646. 13th Year] Wilmington, NC, Tuesday, 23 May 1809, page 3, column 4.

245. PORT OF WILMINGTON. ENTERED, Sch'r Delesdemier, **Tucker**, Boston. Sch'r Vandyck, **Punchard**, Salem. Sch'r Polly, **Lewis**, Beaufort, N.C. Sloop Patty, **Hall**, Charleston. Sch'r Prudentia, **Warner**, Gloucester. Sch'r Ruby, **Wood**, Havana. *Sugar, Coffee, & Molasses, to J. Levy*. Sloop Columbia, **Thompson**, Philad. Sch'r Abagail, **Lafavour**, Beverly. Sch'r Scythian, **Ridding**, Portsmouth, New Hampshire. CLEARED, Brig Equator, **Ingersoll**, Boston. Sch'r Regulator, **M'Ilhenny**, Charleston. Sch'r Azubah & Ruthy, **White**, N. York. Sch'r Mercury, **Ireson**, St. Jago de Cuba. Sch'r Delesdemier, **Tucker**, Boston. Sch'r Polly, **Lewis**, Beaufort, N.C. Brig America, **Shaw**, Providence. Sch'r Prudentia, **Warner**, Gloucester (M.) Sloop Patty, **Hall**, Boston. *The True Republican or American Whig* [Vol. 1. No. 21] Wilmington, NC, Tuesday, 23 May 1809, page 3, column 4. *The Wilmington Gazette* [Number 646. 13th Year] Wilmington, NC, Tuesday, 23 May 1809, page 3, column 4.

246. NOTICE. THE sale of the Ship ROVER, and balance of her CARGO, heretofore advertised to be sold on Wednesday next, is postponed until Saturday the 27th inst. On that day the sale will commence at twelve o'clock, on Captain **Cameron**'s Wharf, on a Credit of two and four Months, for approved indorsed Notes, negotiable at the Bank of Cape Fear, and payable in U. States notes or specie -- or in lieu thereof, Bills with two approved endorsers on Baltimore, Philadelphia, New-York or Boston, ay 60 and 120 days, will be taken. **T. N. GAUTIER**. N.B. The terms of payment for the balance of the cargo on hand will be made known at the sale. May 23. *The True Republican or American Whig* [Vol. 1. No. 21] Wilmington, NC, Tuesday, 23 May 1809, page 3, column 4. *The Wilmington Gazette* [Number 646. 13th Year] Wilmington, NC, Tuesday, 23 May 1809, page 3, column 4.

247. *FIVE DOLLARS REWARD*. RANAWAY from my Plantation at Rocky Point, some Months since, a Negro Man known by the name of **DEMAR**; He is a stout, lusty and ill put together fellow, and walks clumsily, and is between Thirty and Forty years of age, he has been frequently seen in Wilmington, and is supposed is lurking in and about there, as it has became an asylum for Runaways. Whoever shall apprehend and deliver him to Messrs. **Robert** and **William Mitchell**, the Jailor at Wilmington, or to me at Rocky Point, shall received the above Reward, & all reasonable expenses paid. **SAMUEL ASHE**. May 23, 2w. *The True Republican or American Whig* [Vol. 1. No. 21] Wilmington, NC, Tuesday, 23 May 1809, page 3, column 4. *The True Republican or American Whig* [Vol. 1. No. 25] Wilmington, NC, Tuesday, 20 June 1809, page 4, column 2.

248. TEN DOLLARS REWARD. RUNAWAY from the subscriber on the night of the first of this month, a Negro woman named **FLORA**, she is of a yellow complexion and between twenty and twenty-five years of age. I expect she is lurking about Mr. **James Price**'s, on the Sound, or about Mr. **William Jones**'s, near Wilmington. I will give the above reward to any person who will deliver her to me. Captains of vessels and all other persons are cautioned against harboring or

---

[34] A deed of marriage settlement between **Eliza Moore** & **Thomas Mabson** proved by **William McKenzie**, subscribing witness thereto & ordered to be registered. New Hanover County Court of Pleas & Quarter Sessions, Tuesday 22 August 1809, page 281.

concealing said Negro, under the penalty of the law. **ANDREW THALLY**. Duplin County, May 19. tf. *The True Republican or American Whig* [Vol. 1. No. 21] Wilmington, NC, Tuesday, 23 May 1809, page 3, column 4. *The True Republican or American Whig* [Vol. 1. No. 23] Wilmington, NC, Tuesday, 6 June 1809, page 2, column 2. *The True Republican or American Whig* [Vol. 1. No. 25] Wilmington, NC, Tuesday, 20 June 1809, page 4, column 2. *The True Republican or American Whig* [Vol. 1. No. 27] Wilmington, NC, Tuesday, 4 July 1809, page 4, column 3.

249. NOTICE IS HEREBY GIVEN, THAT all the Bonds, Notes and Book accounts due the Subscriber, are assigned to **Thomas Hunter** and **John Foote**, to be collected by them and the amount, together with the proceeds of other property also assigned for that purpose, applied to the discharge of debts due by him. All persons therefore indebted to him, are hereby required to make payment to the said **Thomas Hunter** and **John Foote**, or either of them, as shall be appointed to receive payment so assigned, and all persons having unsettled accounts with him are requested to present them to the above mentioned persons for adjustment. **JOHN WILLIAMS**. May 23 - tf. *The True Republican or American Whig* [Vol. 1. No. 21] Wilmington, NC, Tuesday, 23 May 1809, page 3, column 4. *The Wilmington Gazette* [Number 646. 13th Year] Wilmington, NC, Tuesday, 23 May 1809, page 3, column 4. *The True Republican or American Whig* [Vol. 1. No. 23] Wilmington, NC, Tuesday, 6 June 1809, page 4, column 4. *The True Republican or American Whig* [Vol. 1. No. 25] Wilmington, NC, Tuesday, 20 June 1809, page 4, column 3. *The True Republican or American Whig* [Vol. 1. No. 27] Wilmington, NC, Tuesday, 4 July 1809, page 4, column 3.

250. AGRICULTURAL. *COTTON. The following remarks are by an old experienced Planter of St. Simon, Georgia.* If the land has been recently cleared, or has long remained fallow, turn it up deep in winter; and in the first week in March, bed it up in the following manner -- Form 25 beds in 105 square feet of land, (being the space allotted to each able laborer for a day's work;) this leaves about 4 feet, two and one half inches from the centre of one bed to the centre of the next. The beds should be 3 feet wide, and flat in the middle. About the 15th of March, in the latitude of from 29 to 32, the cultivator should commence sowing, or as it is generally termed, planting. The seed should be well scattered in open trenches, made in the centre of the beds, and covered -- the proportion of seed is one bushel to an acre; this allows for accidents occasioned by worms, or night chills. The cotton should be well weeded by hoes once every twelve days till blown, and even longer, if there is grass, observing to hoe up, that is, to the cotton, till it pods, and hoe down when the cotton is blown, in order to check the growth of the plant. From the proportion of seed mentioned, the cotton plants will come up plentifully, too much so, to suffer all to remain. They should be thinned moderately at each hoeing. When the plants have got strength and growth, which may be about the third hoeing, to disregard worms and bear drought, they should be thinned according to the fertility of the soil, from six inches to near two feet between the stock of plants. In rich river ground the beds should be from five to six feet apart, measuring from centre to centre, and the cotton plants when out of the way of worms, from two to three feet apart. It is advisable to top cotton once or twice in rich low grounds, and also to remove the suckers. The latter end of July is generally considered a proper time for cropping. *Gypsum*, (plaster of Paris) may be used with success on cotton lands *not near the sea*. In river grounds, draining is proper; yet these lands should not be kept too dry. In tide lands, it is beneficial to let the water flow over the lands, without retaining it. In river lands a change of crops is necessary. From actual experiment it has been proved, that river tide lands having the preceding year had rice sown in them, yielded much more cotton the succeeding year then they would have afforded by a continuation of cotton.

     The mere growing of cotton is but a part of the care of the planter; very much depends on classing and cleaning it for market, after it has been housed; sorting before it goes to the jennies; moating and removing any yellow particles, are all essential to assure a preference at a common market of competition. *The True Republican or American Whig* [Vol. 1. No. 21] Wilmington, NC, Tuesday, 23 May 1809, page 4, column 2.

251. PERSIA. *Curious anecdotes from the late travels of M **Gardane**, in Persia*. The politeness of the Persians is of a species perfectly Oriental. A nobleman, of high rank, went one day to the French ambassador's "to bed his pardon because the weather was so bad in Persia."

    The diplomatic conferences at Teheran, are held in the same manner as in our dramatic exhibitions, with the doors open, and in the presence of a multitude of auditors. The Orientals cannot conceive the necessity of secrecy in conventions between states.

    The women are kept as much enslaved in Persia, as in the rest of the east. A Frenchman belonging to the suite of the ambassador, one day, excited a great uproar at Teheran, for having ventured to cast some inquisitive looks at the garden of a seraglio. At the sight of a man, the women uttered screams of affright; some of then even snatched up arms, and prepared to repel ogles with musket balls.

    M. **Gardane** one day asked a Persian nobleman how many children he had? "I don't know," he replied, "enquire of my secretary." The secretary turned to the list, and answered that his master had seventeen children. *The True Republican or American Whig* [Vol. 1. No. 21] Wilmington, NC, Tuesday, 23 May 1809, page 4, column 2.

252. PROPOSAL To publish by subscription, THE *History of the United States*; From the Year 1801 to 1809: The Period During Which THOMAS JEFFERSON directed the affairs of the nation. With an Historical Sketch of the Union, from the commencement of George Washington's Administration… **GEORGE BOURNE**… N.B. As soon as 500 subscribers are obtained the work will be sent to press. April 20. *The True Republican or American Whig* [Vol. 1. No. 21] Wilmington, NC, Tuesday, 23 May 1809, page 4, column 3. *The True Republican or American Whig* [Vol. 1. No. 23] Wilmington, NC, Tuesday, 6 June 1809, page 4, column 4. *The True Republican or American Whig* [Vol. 1. No. 25] Wilmington, NC, Tuesday, 20 June 1809, page 4, column 4. *The True Republican or American Whig* [Vol. 1. No. 27] Wilmington, NC, Tuesday, 4 July 1809, page 4, column 4.

253. A few Boxes Glass. 10 by 12 & 8 by 10, Kegs White lead, Pieces Nankeens, Rheams of Wrapping Paper. **BURGWIN & ORME**. May 9. 3w. *The Wilmington Gazette* [Number 646. 13th Year] Wilmington, NC, Tuesday, 23 May 1809, page 1, column 1.

254. An elegant SMALL SWORD, with a pair of handsome Epaulets, may be purchased on very low terms by applying at this office. *The Wilmington Gazette* [Number 646. 13th Year] Wilmington, NC, Tuesday, 23 May 1809, page 1, column 1.

255. *TO RENT*, That commodious slated Brick House in Front Street and corner of Ewans Alley. It is capable of containing two families with a kitchen to each, &c. **JOHN MARTIN**. February 7. *The Wilmington Gazette* [Number 646. 13th Year] Wilmington, NC, Tuesday, 23 May 1809, page 1, column 2.

256. THE goods lately composing the assortment of **Thomas Wright** will for a short time remain in his possession, to be disposed of at reduced prices, for prompt payment only. **WM. RICHARDSON**. April 18. *The Wilmington Gazette* [Number 646. 13th Year] Wilmington, NC, Tuesday, 23 May 1809, page 1, column 2.

257. NOTICE. AS the subscriber intends to leave the state for a few weeks, he has left his business as respects Books and Accounts in charge of **Peter Maxwell**, Esq., for adjustment, at the counting-house adjoining my dwelling house. **GEORGE CAMERON**. April 11. tf. *The Wilmington Gazette* [Number 646. 13th Year] Wilmington, NC, Tuesday, 23 May 1809, page 1, column 2.

258. RUN-AWAY a Mulatto Boy named **GEORGE**, belonging to the subscriber. As it is probable that he is gone to Wilmington, all masters of vessels and other persons are cautioned, at the peril of the law, which shall be strictly enforced against them, not to harbor or carry him away. Any person who shall deliver the said boy to Messrs. **John Mitchell**, at Wilmington, or **Duncan McRae** of Fayetteville, shall be entitled to a handsome reward. **WILLIAM DUFFY**.

Chatham Court-House. *The Wilmington Gazette* [Number 646. 13th Year] Wilmington, NC, Tuesday, 23 May 1809, page 1 column 2.

259. A SILVER SPOON, Found between the Brick house and Judge **Moore**'s plantation. The owner by proving property, paying for the advertisement and giving a small gratuity to the finder, may have it by applying at this office. May 8. tf. *The Wilmington Gazette* [Number 646. 13th Year] Wilmington, NC, Tuesday, 23 May 1809, page 1, column 3.

260. *From the (Washington) Monitor*. The world's great jubilee is at length arrived, when the hearts of suffering people will be glad by the certain prospects of peace. Old England and America are once more united, and likely to be settled in the solid hands of friendship for ages and for generations to come. And what is to prevent it? . . MENTOR. *The Wilmington Gazette* [Number 646. 13th Year] Wilmington, NC, Tuesday, 23 May 1809, page 1, column 4.

261. *NOTICE*. THE EXECUTORS to the estate of the late **William H. Hill**, Esq., in consequence of the injury already done to the rice-fields (now planted) at Hilton by persons who resort there for the purpose of fishing and fowling, give this public notice, that all persons whatsoever, are positively forbidden to fish or fowl on the rice ground of the said place, on peril of legal prosecution. May 16. tf. *The Wilmington Gazette* [Number 646. 13th Year] Wilmington, NC, Tuesday, 23 May 1809, page 2, column 1.

262. RUNAWAYS. **PETER**, a Mulatto boy, belonging to **A. J. DeROSSET**, about 18 or 19 years of age, low of stature, but sturdy made, bushy hair seldom combed, and inclined generally to be dirty, dressed in striped cotton homespun, tho' he may have other clothes,. **BRYANT SULLIVAN** belonging to **James Telfair**, about 16 years old, also a mulatto, stutters when questioned, a scar across his nose, habited in homespun, but has also other clothes.
   Both these boys have worked several years at the Brick laying business. A reward of ten dollars will be paid by the owner, of the above boys respectively, if taken within the state, and thirty of without the same, and all charges paid, on delivery in Wilmington on their being so secured as that the owners shall get the. Masters of vessels are particularly cautioned against taking them off or harboring them under the penalty of the law, which will be rigidly enforced. **A. J. DeROSSET, JAMES TELFAIR**. May 18. tf. *The Wilmington Gazette* [Number 646. 13th Year] Wilmington, NC, Tuesday, 23 May 1809, page 2, column 1.

263. 30 DOLLARS REWARD. RUN-AWAY from the subscriber on the eleventh instant *THREE NEGRO MEN*, belonging to the estate of Capt. **John Green**, named *Moses, Harry*, and *Carolina*. **MOSES** is a stout, able, and likely fellow, about five feet ten inches high, very large eyes, about 22 years of age and speaks very distinct, not very dark; had on blue dyed homespun pantaloons, blue Negro cloth jacket. **HARRY** is a very likely fellow, about 21 years of age, five feet 8 inches high, very dark skin, pleasing countenance, had on a glossed servant's hat, dressed in blue Negro cloth, and wears his hair platted before and behind. **CAROLINA** is about 28 years old, slender made, narrow long face, swings himself very much when he walks, about five feet seven inches high and homely. Thirty Dollars will be paid for apprehending said Negros and securing them in any goal, or ten dollars for each and if delivered to the subscriber in addition all necessary expenses paid. All persons forewarned from harboring said Negroes or masters of vessels from carrying them off under the penalty of the law. **JOHN GRANGE**. Brunswick County, N.C. Town Creek, May 13, 1809} tf. *The Wilmington Gazette* [Number 646. 13th Year] Wilmington, NC, Tuesday, 23 May 1809, page 2, column 1.

264. Ran-away, a likely Negro fellow, named **TOM**, formerly owned by Mr. **Lucas** at the White Marsh. He is about 5 feet 8 or 9 inches high and well made. Having a Wife here and a Mother on Town Creek, he may probably be lurking about Town. All Masters of vessels and other persons are therefore cautioned at the peril of the law (which shall be strictly enforced against them) not

to harbor or carry him away. Whoever shall deliver the said Fellow to the Subscriber, or lodge him in jail, shall receive 15 dollars. **HENRY YOUNG**. May 9. *The Wilmington Gazette* [Number 646. 13th Year] Wilmington, NC, Tuesday, 23 May 1809, page 2, column 1.

265. *AN OVERSEER WANTED*, Who understand the culture of RICE, is willing to superintend a gang of from 12 to 15 hands, and bears a good character. Liberal terms will be given. Apply at his Office. May 9. tf. *The Wilmington Gazette* [Number 646. 13th Year] Wilmington, NC, Tuesday, 23 May 1809, page 2, column 1.

266. FOR RENT, at a low rate, that dry and convenient CELLAR under my Book Store. **W. S. HASELL**. *The Wilmington Gazette* [Number 646. 13th Year] Wilmington, NC, Tuesday, 23 May 1809, page 2, column 1.

267. *From the Boston Repertory*. Candid reflections on the important event which has brightened the prospects of United America and evinced a change in her national policy. . . The mere satisfaction of showing the supporters of Mr. **Jefferson** and his wretched policy, that the glory they claim from his measures is ridiculous, would not be worth our attention. . . *The Wilmington Gazette* [Number 646. 13th Year] Wilmington, NC, Tuesday, 23 May 1809, page 2, columns 2 & 3.

268. Norfolk, May 12, 1809. Arrived this morning the schooner *Catherine Shepherd, Capt. Webb*, in 11 days from St. Bartholomew's, he left there about 250 sail of American vessels; flour nine to ten dollars per barrel. *The Wilmington Gazette* [Number 646. 13th Year] Wilmington, NC, Tuesday, 23 May 1809, page 2, column 3.

269. ENCOURAGEMENT TO GO ON. If Mr. **Madison** has firmness to persist in the laudable measures which he has begun, he will be supported by all the federal republicans in congress, and will succeed in the system he adopts; but if he shrinks from his duty and abandons the noble position he has taken, at every step he will have to combat a formidable opposition, he will be embarrassed in all his operations, and be finally defeated in his objects. *The Wilmington Gazette* [Number 646. 13th Year] Wilmington, NC, Tuesday, 23 May 1809, page 3, column 2.

270. COMMUNICATION. "Neither can we trust thee, Mentor, when thou wouldest counsel us to ally ourselves to France, seeking from her, friendship, officers and arms; nor when thou wouldest make us believe that we are all Englishmen - All Americans." Changes in a political course are often singular, great and sudden. In no public journal has this remark been more strikingly verified than in the "Monitor" nor in any writer more glaringly realized than in "Mentor," who appears to hold a conspicuous station in its columns. . . AN OBSERVER. *The Wilmington Gazette* [Number 646. 13th Year] Wilmington, NC, Tuesday, 23 May 1809, page 3, column 2.

271. The Duke of York has resigned the office of commander in chief of the British forces, and Sir **Harry Dundas** now acts in that capacity. It is expected that the authority will soon be placed in the hands of commissioners. *The Wilmington Gazette* [Number 646. 13th Year] Wilmington, NC, Tuesday, 23 May 1809, page 3, column 2.

272. The Commissioners of South Carolina, having refused to meet those of this state, to settle the dividing line, our Commissioners did not deem it necessary to go. We learn, however, the Rev. **Joseph Caldwell** of the University, the Artist on the part of this state, proceeded to the place of meeting and ascertained the 35th degree of latitude. One of the South-Carolina Commissioners we learn, had resigned, which may have caused the others not to act. *Minerva*. *The Wilmington Gazette* [Number 646. 13th Year] Wilmington, NC, Tuesday, 23 May 1809, page 3, column 2.

273. TIMBER. It has been long known in some parts of Europe, that taking off the bar as far up the trees as it can conveniently be done, and let them stand till the following autumn or winter, before they are cut down, is a means of making the timber much stronger and more durable, than

it otherwise would be. It is more suitable for all kinds of carriages and instruments of husbandry, as well as for fences. Its greater durability has not yet been ascertained by the writers, but that it is otherwise improved has been tested. It has been asserted by persons of credit, that in some parts of the United States, where pine timber abounds, the farmers are in the practice of barking the pine as far up as is necessary for a fence post; in this state they are suffered to stand until dead. The trees are then cut down, and the part which has been barked will be found saturated with turpentine and thereby rendered remarkably durable for posts or fences. *The Wilmington Gazette* [Number 646. 13th Year] Wilmington, NC, Tuesday, 23 May 1809, page 3, column 3.

274. The Schooner Corotoman, Capt. **Taylor**, from Philadelphia, out about ten days, was wrecked on the beach near Topsail Sound, about 12 miles from Wilmington, on Sunday evening the 20th inst., about 10 o'clock - cargo French Brandy Rum, Flour, Dry Goods, & c., consigned to **R. W. Brown**. *The Wilmington Gazette* [Number 646. 13th Year] Wilmington, NC, Tuesday, 23 May 1809, page 3, column 3.

275. There will be a CONCERT of the HARMONIC SOCIETY, To-mor-row Evening. Tickets to be had at the Book-Store of *W. S. HASELL*. May 23. *The Wilmington Gazette* [Number 646. 13th Year] Wilmington, NC, Tuesday, 23 May 1809, page 3, column 3.

276. *NOTICE.* WHEREAS I am frequently out of town, I have authorized **William Nutt**, Sheriff; to take up such Jurors Certificates and claims on the county as may be presented for payment. **ALLMAND HALL**, *C. Treasurer*. May 23. 2w. *The Wilmington Gazette* [Number 646. 13th Year] Wilmington, NC, Tuesday, 23 May 1809, page 3, column 3.

277. The Proposals for the Circulating Library, with a Catalogue of the Books composing it, may be seen by applying to *W. S. HASELL*. *The Wilmington Gazette* [Number 646. 13th Year] Wilmington, NC, Tuesday, 23 May 1809, page 3, column 3.

278. FOR PHILADELPHIA, The Schooner *HARMONY*, **Richard Lucas** Master; Will positively sail on Thursday next. For freight of a few bales of Cotton, under deck, or passage apply to the Master on board, or to Mr. **E. WINSLOW**. *The Wilmington Gazette* [Number 646. 13th Year] Wilmington, NC, Tuesday, 23 May 1809, page 3, column 4.

279. **WILLIAM DICK**, Has the honor of informing his friends and the public that having lately been appointed to the office of Inspector of Naval Stores for this port, in that capacity he will be happy to serve them. He trusts, that it is unnecessary for him to make assurances, of the principles which he will of course govern his conduct, a readiness to attend to the duties of his office and fidelity in the performance of them. Where he meets with employment he will endeavor to deserve and will gratefully acknowledge it. May 23. tf. *The Wilmington Gazette* [Number 646. 13th Year] Wilmington, NC, Tuesday, 23 May 1809, page 3, column 4. June 3. *The True Republican or American Whig* [Vol. 1. No. 23] Wilmington, NC, Tuesday, 6 June 1809, page 3, column 3. *The True Republican or American Whig* [Vol. 1. No. 25] Wilmington, NC, Tuesday, 20 June 1809, page 4, column 3. *The True Republican or American Whig* [Vol. 1. No. 27] Wilmington, NC, Tuesday, 4 July 1809, page 4, column 3.

280. *TEN DOLLARS REWARD.* RANAWAY from Mr. **John Williams**, in Wilmington, about the first of April, 1808, a Negro woman named **JESSA**, about 23 years of age, 5 feet 5 inches high, slender made, and likely; dresses very genteelly, and generally wears a blue handkerchief on her head, which comes down over her eyes, on account of their being very weak; She is light complected, was brought up in the family of Mr. **Daniel Mallet**, is a tolerable good Seamstress, and is very well acquainted with house work. Having purchased the above Negro wench some time ago from Mr. **J. Williams**, I will give the above Reward for delivering her to me, or the Jailor of this place, or any other in the State. Is she will return to me in the course of two or three months from this time, I will give her the liberty of procuring another master, provided she does not wish to live with me, or hiring her own time. **THOMAS HUNTER**. May 30. *The True*

Republican or American Whig [Vol. 1. No. 23] Wilmington, NC, Tuesday, 6 June 1809, page 2, column 2. *The True Republican or American Whig* [Vol. 1. No. 25] Wilmington, NC, Tuesday, 20 June 1809, page 1, column 1. *The True Republican or American Whig* [Vol. 1. No. 27] Wilmington, NC, Tuesday, 4 July 1809, page 4, column 3. *The True Republican or American Whig* [Vol. 1. No. 45] Wilmington, NC, Tuesday, 7 November 1809, page 3, column 4.

281. THE EXHIBITION *OF THE WONDERFUL CURIOSITIES* May be seen in this town for a short time, Consisting of *A Shepherd and Shepherdess, and their Child; also a Sheep, Lamb, and Lap-Dog. Their dress consists of Glass that is plaited, and as fine as silk.* Also A PANORAMA, *OF VARIOUS CITIES, viz.* The Cities of London, Paris, Madrid, Lisbon, Rome, Venice and St. Petersburgh; the battle of Trafalgar, Lord Nelson in his last dying moments. The above Exhibition is allowed to be one of the greatest curiosities ever displayed in the United States. *The Exhibition to conclude with* THE PHANTASMAGORIA. Admittance for adults, 50 cents; Children 25 cents. Hours of admission from 9 o'clock in the morning, until 10 o'clock at night. June 3. *The True Republican or American Whig* [Vol. 1. No. 23] Wilmington, NC, Tuesday, 6 June 1809, page 3, column 3.

282. *NOTICE.* PERRY & FONTAINE, on Market-wharf, inform the public, that in addition to their old stock, they have received from Charleston, some fresh and well adapted GOODS for the season -- viz. Cotton Cambers and Shirting, Calicoes, Ginghams, Blue and Yellow Nankeens, German & English Oznaburgs, Threads, Patent Sewing Cotton, Turkey Red, Straw and Willow Bonnets, Crockery Ware, with sundry articles too numerous to mention. They have also a large assortment of Groceries, Old Cognac Brandy and Gin, 4th proof Jamaica Rum, a few barrels of country Brandy and Whiskey, and two hundred barrels of Flour, which they will dispose of low for cash, or notes at sixty days, negotiable at the Bank. June 5. 6w. *The True Republican or American Whig* [Vol. 1. No. 23] Wilmington, NC, Tuesday, 6 June 1809, page 3, column 3. *The True Republican or American Whig* [Vol. 1. No. 25] Wilmington, NC, Tuesday, 20 June 1809, page 3, column 4. *The True Republican or American Whig* [Vol. 1. No. 27] Wilmington, NC, Tuesday, 4 July 1809, page 3, column 4.

283. JUST ARRIVED. *Per the Sloop Morning Star, Capt.* **Owens**, *and for sale by* **R. W. BROWN**, 5 pieces Oznaburgs, 10 pieces Cotton Bagging, 1 ton Bar Iron, 20 bbls superfine Philadelphia Flour, 12 kegs Crackers, 5 barrels Beer. June 3. *The True Republican or American Whig* [Vol. 1. No. 23] Wilmington, NC, Tuesday, 6 June 1809, page 3, column 3. *The True Republican or American Whig* [Vol. 1. No. 25] Wilmington, NC, Tuesday, 20 June 1809, page 3, column 4.

284. *J.* **JENNETT**, Respectfully thanks the inhabitants of Wilmington, for the encouragement they have given him as a teacher, and informs them that his relaxed state of health constrains him to relinquish that occupation. The school, not withstanding, will be continued under the direction of Mr. **Forster**, who will teach Latin, Geography, English Grammar, Arithmetic, & c. on the usual terms. June 3. *The True Republican or American Whig* [Vol. 1. No. 23] Wilmington, NC, Tuesday, 6 June 1809, page 3, column 3.

285. *FOR SALE*: Bar IRON, Jamaica Rum, Country Gin, Sugar in Hhds, Wine in pipes, Porter in tierces, Whiskey, Philadelphia Beef, Fayetteville Beef, Flour, Pork, A few hhds prime Tobacco, Ship Bread in biscuits, Crackers in kegs, Raisins in boxes, Tin Ware, 1 bbl Confectionary, rock Candy by the box, Almonds. **ROBERT W. BROWN**. May 29. 3w. *The True Republican or American Whig* [Vol. 1. No. 23] Wilmington, NC, Tuesday, 6 June 1809, page 3, column 3. *The True Republican or American Whig* [Vol. 1. No. 25] Wilmington, NC, Tuesday, 20 June 1809, page 4, column 3.

286. TAKEN UP, AT the four mile House, by the subscriber, on the 30th ult, a dark brown STEER, the right ear marked with a swallow-fork, and the left eat with the swallow-fork and hole -- branded on the rear rump with an S, and the ends of his horns sawed off. The said Steer has been valued by two free-holders, at twelve-dollars, and I have slaughtered him. The owner, by proving the property, paying charges, and applying to me, shall receive the valuation. **J. E. HOBBS**. Wilmington, June 3. *The True Republican or American Whig* [Vol. 1. No. 23] Wilmington, NC, Tuesday, 6 June 1809, page 3, column 3. *The True Republican or American Whig* [Vol. 1. No. 25] Wilmington, NC, Tuesday, 20 June 1809, page 4, column 3.

287. THE TRUE REPUBLICAN. WILMINGTON, TUESDAY, JUNE 6, 1809. The ship Herkimer, arrived at N. York, from London, brings London papers to the 29th March. The following embraces the most prominent articles of intelligence: A revolution has occurred in Sweden, which has issued in the deposition of **Gustavus**, and the seizure of the reins of government by his uncle, the duke of Sundermania, who has publicly declared his nephew incapable of conducting the affairs of the nation. The French are said to have retired from the Tagus, and some advantages to have been gained by the Spaniards. 180,000 French soldiers were in Germany, but hostilities had not commenced between France and Austria. No information has been received of the part which Russia means to take. It is reported that **Massena** has been killed by **Bonaparte** in a fit of passion, though other accounts say it was an accident. A London print states that Sir **David Dundas** is appointed commander in chief of the British armies. Gen. **Wilkinson** arrived at New-Orleans on the 13th of April. As a proof of his high worth and eminent services, a splendid entertainment was given on the occasion. *The True Republican or American Whig* [Vol. 1. No. 23] Wilmington, NC, Tuesday, 6 June 1809, page 3, column 4.

288. Mr. **JOHN ADAMS** seems determined to ruin the *Junta* by *writing down* their favorite dogmas of *submission* to England and *hostility* to France. We heartily wish he may persevere in his labors. . . *Baltimore Evening Post*. *The True Republican or American Whig* [Vol. 1. No. 23] Wilmington, NC, Tuesday, 6 June 1809, page 3, column 4.

289. PORT OF WILMINGTON. *ENTERED*. Sch'r Regulator, **M'Ilhenny**, Charleston, _____, **Hull**, Harwick. Sch'r Eagle, **Sikes**, New-River. Sch'r Polly, **Jarvis**, New-River. Sch'r Rover, **Whitby**, New-River. Brig Fortitude, **Minotti**, St. Bartholomew's. Sch'r Little John, **Capps**, New-River. Sch'r Betsy, **Wilson**, New-river. Sloop Hunter, **Mayden**, Nantucket. Sch'r Milly, **Rhodes**, Charleston [SC]. Sch'r Return, **Garrett**, New-River. Sch'r Harriet, **Grafton**, Providence. Sloop Morning Star, **Owens**, Philadelphia. Sch'r Venus, **Wadham**, New-York. Sch'r Comet, **Jenkins**, New-York. Sch'r Heart of Oak, **Hall**, Boston. Sch'r Nancy, **Braston**, Swansborough. Sch'r Tryall, **Chase**, Boston. *CLEARED*. Brig Sally, **Bernard**, Boston. Sch'r Abigail, **Lefavour**, Beverly, (M.). Sch'r Scythian, **Reddings**, Portsmouth. Snow Fanny, **Anderson**, St. Bartholomew's. Sch'r Betsy, **Wilson**, Charleston. Sch'r Regulator, **M'Ilhenny**, Charleston. Sch'r Rover, **Whitby**, New-River. Sch'r Eagle, **Sikes**, New-River. Sch'r Little John, **Capps**, New-River. Sch'r Return, **Garrett**, New-River. *The True Republican or American Whig* [Vol. 1. No. 23] Wilmington, NC, Tuesday, 6 June 1809, page 3, column 4.

290. PUBLIC DINNER, *On the 10th of June*. ALL those who are disposed to celebrate the revival of COMMERCE, which will take place on the tenth instant, are requested to subscribe their names for a Public Dinner, to be given on that day. A subscription paper is left at the Book-Store of **W. S. Hasell**, and at the office of the True Republican. June 5. *The True Republican or American Whig* [Vol. 1. No. 23] Wilmington, NC, Tuesday, 6 June 1809, page 3, column 4.

291. *SIXTY DOLLARS REWARD*. RAN AWAY from the Subscriber, living on Bay River, Craven County, North-Carolina, two Negro Fellows, named **BOB** and **LUKE**. **Bob**, who sometimes call himself **Jack**, is about 5 feet 3 or 6 inches high, is of a yellow complexion, stoops a little when walking and speaks tolerable good English; had on when he went off, a thick grey cloth jacket, without any buttons, but probably he may have shifted his dress. **LUKE** is rather taller than **Bob**, alias **Jack**, and of a deeper black, has thick lips, and had on a thick grey cloth jacket, but as they had all their clothes with them, nothing is more likely than they may have shifted their outside dress, and perhaps they may endeavor to pass for free men. Whoever will secure them in any jail and give the owner notice, so that he may get them again, shall have the above reward of 60 dollars, or 30 dollars for either of them. It is not unlikely they may make for some seaport town, and endeavor to get on board some vessel bound to sea, masters of vessels,

therefore, and all other persons, are hereby forbidden to take them on board, harbor or in any wise conceal them, under the penalty of the law. **RICHARD CRUTCH.** April 8. 4w. *The True Republican or American Whig* [Vol. 1. No. 23] Wilmington, NC, Tuesday, 6 June 1809, page 3, column 4. *The True Republican or American Whig* [Vol. 1. No. 25] Wilmington, NC, Tuesday, 20 June 1809, page 1, column 1. *The True Republican or American Whig* [Vol. 1. No. 27] Wilmington, NC, Tuesday, 4 July 1809, page 4, column 3.

292. SHIPWRECK, & C. We stated in a former paper, that the ship Monticello, from Lima, fell in with the wreck of a vessel at sea on which was found a man, the last of the crew, who had preserved a precarious existence for a number of days by feeding upon the bodies of his comrades. This statement in the first instance was considered to extravagant to be true; but it is now known to be a fact. It was also said that the crew cast lots, which of them should die, to sustain the lives of the remainder; but this is not confirmed by the narrative of the survivor. He admits, however, that when any of his comrades died from hunger of thirst he was driven to the necessity of existing upon their remains. When the captain of the Monticello took this wrecked man on board his ship, he gave him a change of cloths and linen, and would not suffer him to take much sustenance at one time. The first nutriment he gave him was two cups of coffee and a small piece of toast and by adhering to this system in the course of a few days, the man was quite restored to health. He proved a most excellent sailor, and was a great acquisition. But it is a curious fact that not one of the crew of the Monticello would for a length of time, associate with him, on account of the diet he had fed upon. Hoping to cure them of their prejudice, the captain kindly invited the unfortunate seamen to his table, but this had not the desired effect, on the contrary, those persons who usually messed with the captain deserted his table. Time, however, and the general good conduct of the man, restored him to the society of his shipmates. In relating to them his sufferings on board the wreck, he abstained as much as possible from mentioning the matter of his subsistence; but the crew themselves had witnessed his food hung up in the shrouds at the time he was taken from the wreck. Particulars given by the wrecked mariner are these: his name is **Thomas Moorhead**, a native of the county of Durham; he served his time to the seas in the coal trade; the ship in which he was wrecked was the Acorn, Captain **M'Leod**, of Stocton, to which they were bound from America, when on the 30th Oct., a severe gale of wind came on, in which the ship made a great deal of water, and finally filled and overset, in lat. 51, long. 48, by which misfortune, the carpenter and a black man were drowned. In about ten minutes the sea carried away the mainmast and she righted again. At this period the sea made a clear passage over the ship, but she could not well sink, being laden with timber. The master, **Andrew Brass**, and **John Sampson**, a boy, were washed overboard, but at day light the master was washed on board again, having been for some hours clinging to the pieces of the wreck. All hands proceeded to the foretop, and in five hours time two more of the crew died in consequence of the inclemency of the weather. Soon after the timber man, **Francis Bradly**, **Christopher Baly** and **Thomas Bales**, boys, nearly whole of the remainder of the hands, were frost bitten. In this deplorable situation they all remained in the top four days, when not a fragment of the cabin was to be seen. Everything was washed out of the cabin windows, except three pieces of meat, which were found in the stern sheets. The ship's rudder parted on the 12th of November. **Thomas Charlton**, and the boy **Charles English**, died on the 23d. The master prolonged a miserable existence to the eleventh Dec. on which day he died. **William Pearson** fell a victim to thirst. All the water casks were swept off the deck when the vessel upset on the 31st.; the little moisture they procured was from the rain that fell, and which they caught in their hats, & c, in the foretop. The Monticello fell in with the wreck of the Acorn, in lat. 41, long. 25, when the captain immediately sent a longboat for **Moorhead**. He was taken out of the top where he had been *fifty-one* days, and towards the latter end expecting to share the unhappy fate of his companions. *N. Y. Even. Post. The True Republican or American Whig* [Vol. 1. No. 23] Wilmington, NC, Tuesday, 6 June 1809, page 4, columns 2 & 3.

293. REMARKABLE FUNERAL. On Sunday last was interred, in the burial ground of St. Martin in-the-fields, the remains of **Hugh Hewson**, who died at the advanced age of 85. . . He

was no less the personage then the identical Hugh Strap, whom Doctor **Smollet** has rendered so conspicuously interesting in his life & adventures of Roderic Random[35], and for upwards of forty years had kept a hairdresser's shop in the above parish. . . We understand the deceased the deceased has left behind him an interlined copy of Roderick Random pointing out the facts, showing how far they were indebted to the genius of the doctor, & to which extent they were bottomed in reality. . . Of late years he was employed as keeper of the promenade in Villier's Walk, Adelphi, and was much noticed and respected by the inhabitants who frequented that place. *London paper. The True Republican or American Whig* [Vol. 1. No. 23] Wilmington, NC, Tuesday, 6 June 1809, page 4, column 3.

294. *Just received from Philadelphia, and for sale at the office of the True Republican*, Letter Paper, by the quire or ream, Do. Superfine Vellum Post, Pewter Inkstands, Ink-Powder, and Wafers. Also, Pocket-Books, of different sizes. *The True Republican or American Whig* [Vol. 1. No. 23] Wilmington, NC, Tuesday, 6 June 1809, page 4, column 3. *The True Republican or American Whig* [Vol. 1. No. 25] Wilmington, NC, Tuesday, 20 June 1809, page 4, column 4.

295. To the Editor of the Enquirer. *SIR*, The conduct of those amongst us, who attempt to rob the late administration of the well earned fame acquired by the change in our foreign relations, affords a signal instance of ingratitude. . . As to our government, an adjustment founded on such principles and produced by such causes as have been described, will form on of the proudest and most lasting monuments of its glory. PUBLIUS. *The True Republican or American Whig* [Vol. 1. No. 25] Wilmington, NC, Tuesday, 20 June 1809, page 1, columns 2 & 3.

296. *FROM LATE LONDON PAPERS*. London, April 9. *Sir **John Moore**'s celebrated last letter*. Yesterday we were favored with a copy of the following letter of sir **John Moore**, which has just been printed in pursuance of the order of the house of commons, and concerning which great curiosity has been excited. Extract of a letter from lieut. general sir **John Moore**, to Viscount Castlereagh, dated Corunna, January 12, 1809. . . *The True Republican or American Whig* [Vol. 1. No. 25] Wilmington, NC, Tuesday, 20 June 1809, page 2, columns 1 & 2.

297. *Affairs of Austria*. Report speaks of a treaty of peace having been signed between Russian and Turkey, affected through the mediation of Austria, and the emperor Alexander has put in motion an army for the protection of the Austrian territories. . . *The True Republican or American Whig* [Vol. 1. No. 25] Wilmington, NC, Tuesday, 20 June 1809, page 2, column 2.

298. CONGRESS. *House of Representatives. Friday, June 2*. Mr. Montgomery presented a petition from distillers and others, citizens of the United States, praying Congress to prohibit the importation of spirits, distilled from grain, and to impose much higher duties on distillation materials. Referred to the committee of Commerce and Manufactures. . . *Monday, June 5*. A message was received from the Senate, informing the house of the death of the honorable **Francis Malborne**, Senator from the state of Rhode Island, & c. On motion of Mr. **Potter**, *resolved unanimously*, that the members of this House do wear crape on the left arm for the space for one month, in testimony of their respect for the memory of the deceased. . . *The True Republican or American Whig* [Vol. 1. No. 25] Wilmington, NC, Tuesday, 20 June 1809, page 2, column 3.

299. THE TRUE REPUBLICAN. WILMINGTON, TUESDAY, JUNE 20, 1809. It is said that the American ships detained at Algeciras, have been released, and have sailed from thence. Payment has been received for such part of their cargoes as had not been taken by the

---

[35] **Tobias George Smollett** (1721-1771), *The Adventures of Roderick Random* published as fiction in 1749. Roderick's companion through most of the novel is Hugh Strap, a simple-hearted barber's apprentice and former schoolmate of Roderick's. The two end up serving twice on British ships, once on a privateer and once on a warship.

government. - The ship Eliza Ann, captain **Burr**, arrived at New-York on the 5th inst. in 40 days from Cadiz. Captain **Burr** informs us verbally, says a New-York paper, that on the morning he sailed from Cadiz, an express arrived there from Seville and that the Junta were removing to Cadiz. . . The brig Julian, Capt. **Williams**, arrived at Boston on the 4th inst. in 40 days from Lisbon, Accounts received by this arrival, state that the French had not made any movements towards Lisbon -- that Sir **David Beard** had just arrived with 7000 troops from England, which increased the British forces on that station to twenty-five thousand. . . The Sloop of War, the Enterprize, says the National Intelligencer, will sail without delay from the port of New-York for Holland, and will be stationed off the Texel, to afford information to the commanders of the merchant vessels of the United States, as to the ports of Holland and of the North of Europe, to which they may safely proceed with their cargoes. *The True Republican or American Whig* [Vol. 1. No. 25] Wilmington, NC, Tuesday, 20 June 1809, page 3, column 1.

300. *To "A Federalist," Editor on particular emergencies of the Wilmington Gazette.* Sir, As long as hot-headed, shallow brained politicians confine their nonsensical stuff to the common chat of the day, they who would stoop to reply to or contradict their stupidity, would evince as much folly as the blockheads themselves. . . Wishing you more truth and brains, less fibbing and foolishness, I bid you adieu, A REPUBLICAN. *The True Republican or American Whig* [Vol. 1. No. 25] Wilmington, NC, Tuesday, 20 June 1809, page 3, columns 2 & 3.

301. **Edward Lloyd**, Esq. has been chosen Governor of Maryland, vic **Robert Wright** resigned. *The True Republican or American Whig* [Vol. 1. No. 25] Wilmington, NC, Tuesday, 20 June 1809, page 3, column 3.

302. It is with sensations of painful regret that we announce the sudden death of **Francis Malborne**, Esq. a Senator from the state of Rhode-Island. He dropped down yesterday on his way to attend Divine Services at the Capitol, and immediately expired. *N. Intel. The True Republican or American Whig* [Vol. 1. No. 25] Wilmington, NC, Tuesday, 20 June 1809, page 3, column 3.

303. PORT OF WILMINGTON. *ENTERED*. Ship Bedford, **Dennin**, Portsmouth. Sloop Betsy, **Pearce**, Newport. Sch'r Charlotte, **Cartwright**, Charleston. Sch'r Regulator, **M'ilhenny**, Charleston. Brig Iris, **Smith**, Charleston. Brig Claris, **M'lean**, Charleston. Sch'r polly, **Grant**, Swansborough. *CLEARED*. Sch'r heart of oak, **Hall**, Liverpool. Sch'r Venus, **Wadham**, New-York. Sch'r Buonaparte, **Chairis**, Shalotte. Sloop Columbia, **Allen**, Newport. Sloop Charlotte, **Cartwright**, Nantucket. Sch'r Triall, **Chase**, Antigua. Sch'r Regulator, **M'ilhenny**, Charleston. *The True Republican or American Whig* [Vol. 1. No. 25] Wilmington, NC, Tuesday, 20 June 1809, page 3, column 3.

304. TWO APPRENTICES WANTED. *To the Gold and Silver Smith's business*; WHO will also be taught the knowledge of Watch repairing, if required. **N. DANA**. June 20. *The True Republican or American Whig* [Vol. 1. No. 25] Wilmington, NC, Tuesday, 20 June 1809, page 3, column 3. *The True Republican or American Whig* [Vol. 1. No. 27] Wilmington, NC, Tuesday, 4 July 1809, page 2, column 2.

305. TO THE PUBLIC. THE Subscriber offers his services in the *Commission and Factorage line,* and will pay strict attention to the interest of those who may favor him with their commands. His charges for commissions, storage, &c shall be very reasonable. Rice planters, especially, may find it to their interest to employ a factor: and from his experience in business, he flatters himself he will be enabled to transact the business of County Merchants to their satisfactions. **A. LAZARUS**. Wilmington, June 12. 3w. *The True Republican or American Whig* [Vol. 1. No. 25] Wilmington, NC, Tuesday, 20 June 1809, page 3, column 3. *The True Republican or American Whig* [Vol. 1. No. 27] Wilmington, NC, Tuesday, 4 July 1809, page 4, column 2.

306. NOTICE. ON Tuesday, the 27th instant, will be sold at Public Auction, in Wilmington, for gold or silver coin, the Schooner called the *ISABELLA*, of about 138 tons burthen, with her Tackle, Furniture, & c. for the benefit of the United States, and ordered to be sold by a decree of

the honorable the District Court of Cape-Fear. **JUNIUS C. DUNBIBIN**, *D. M.* June 1. *The True Republican or American Whig* [Vol. 1. No. 25] Wilmington, NC, Tuesday, 20 June 1809, page 3, column 3.

307. NOTICE. ON Tuesday, the 27th inst. will be sold at Public Auction, in Wilmington, for gold or silver coin, the Schooner called the *DOLPHIN*, of about 87 tons burthen, with her Tackel, Furniture, & c. agreeable to a decree of the Honorable the District Court of Cape-Fear. **J. C. DUNBIBIN**, *D. M.* June 1. *The True Republican or American Whig* [Vol. 1. No. 25] Wilmington, NC, Tuesday, 20 June 1809, page 3, column 4.

308. *To the FREEMEN and ELECTORS Of New-Hanover County. Fellow Citizens*, I TAKE this method to acquaint you, that I am a candidate for the Commons in the next General Assembly, for the county of New-Hanover. Being truly conscious, Gentlemen, that there are many addresses to you of this nature at this time. I pretend not to offer or plead any personal merit, my public and private character is no doubt, sufficiently known, to enable you to determine whether you can place your confidence in me, or not. Should I receive a majority of your approbations, my time and small talents shall be devoted to your services and the good of the community at large. I have the honor, Gentlemen, Of being your obed't serv't, **DAVID JONES**. Black River, June 11. *The True Republican or American Whig* [Vol. 1. No. 25] Wilmington, NC, Tuesday, 20 June 1809, page 3, column 4.

309. *From the Public Advertiser*. To the Editors. *New-Orleans, April 29, 1809.* "Previous to General **Wilkinson**'s arrival here, the relics of **Clarke**'s and **Burr**'s adherents assembled to their utmost force, and devised every plan in their power to dishonest the man, who had elected, exposed and defeated their flagitious designs against the happiness and repose of our country. . . *The True Republican or American Whig* [Vol. 1. No. 25] Wilmington, NC, Tuesday, 20 June 1809, page 4, column 2.

310. PEACH TREE. The following useful information is communicated for publication, for the benefit of those who are in the habit of propagating the peach tree, by a gentleman of Newport, R. I. who had been twice in South America: The preventative against the ravages of the insects which infect the peach tree in South America, is simply binding a piece of raw hide around the trunk of the tree, just above the surface of the earth. The hair side of the hide is placed outwards. *The True Republican or American Whig* [Vol. 1. No. 25] Wilmington, NC, Tuesday, 20 June 1809, page 4, column 2.

311. TWENTY DOLLARS, WILL be given by the subscriber, for taking up and confining in jail, or delivering to him, the following runaways, or TEN DOLLARS for either of them - viz. *YORKSHIRE*, a likely young fellow, about five feet, nine or ten inches high, rather slim, straight, and well made; wears his hair queued and platted. He formerly belonged to Mr. **George Merrick**, deceased; is well known in Wilmington, on the Sound, and Rocky Point; and has a wife belonging to Miss **Howe**, near Wilmington, by whom he is no doubt harboured. *JUPITER* or *JUBE*, a very small fellow, about five feet high, twenty-one or twenty-two years old; has thick lips and small eyes. He runaway on the night of the 22d ultimo, and stole a horse, a double barrel gun, and a pair of boots. The horse was found the next morning on this side of New River. **Jupitor** formerly belonged to Mr. **Richard Roberts**, on White-Oak, and lately to Mr. **William Hadnot** of Onslow County. He has a wife belonging to Mr. **Cooper Huggins**, on the north-east branch of New River; his mother is owned by Mr. **Frederick Foy,** near Newbern, and he has a sister at Mr. **Daniel Newton**'s, at the mouth of Wallace's Creek, in Onslow County. It is supposed he will harbor at some one or all of the above mentioned places, or on French's neck, where he is well known. **ALLMAND HALL**. *Sloop Point, New-Hanover*, *June* 4. *The True Republican or American Whig* [Vol. 1. No. 25] Wilmington, NC, Tuesday, 20 June 1809, page 4, column 2.

312. CONGRESS. *House of Representatives*. Friday, June 16. The question pending at the time of adjournment yesterday, that the committee have leave to sit again on the bill supplementary to the act for the support of public credit, & c. was carried, 52 to 36; and on motion of Mr. **Eppes**,

the House resolved itself into a committee of the whole on the subject. Mr. **Pitkin** in the chair...
The True Republican or American Whig [Vol. 1. No. 27] Wilmington, NC, Tuesday, 4 July 1809, page 2, column 4.

313. FOR NEW-YORK, *The Schooner AMANDA*, Captain **Magrath**, to sail on the 11th Instant, for *Freight* or *Passage*, apply to **HANSON KELLY**. July 4. *The True Republican or American Whig* [Vol. 1. No. 27] Wilmington, NC, Tuesday, 4 July 1809, page 2, column 4.

314. *Just received from Philadelphia, and for sale at the office of the True Republican*, Lotter paper, by the quire or ream, Do. Superfine Vellum Post, Pew er Inkstands, Ink-Powder, and Wafers, Also, Pocket-Books, of different sizes. *The True Republican or American Whig* [Vol. 1. No. 27] Wilmington, NC, Tuesday, 4 July 1809, page 2, column 4.

315. THE TRUE REPUBLICAN. *WILMINGTON*, Tuesday, July 4, 1809. It appears that considerable preparations have been making the different parts of the Union, to celebrate the Anniversary of American Independence... A letter from St. Bartholomew's, June 3, says, We have most dreadful accounts of an insurrection of the blacks at Jamaica, two-thirds of which island are said to be in their possession. The troops are going down from Martinique to assist in suppressing the insurgents. [This news is contradicted in another print.] ... Capt. **Lake** of the Flora, from N. Orleans, (arrived at N: York) informs, that the French consul at that place, had applied to the Governor for the privilege of landing 18,000 French inhabitants, who had been ordered to leave Cuba, which request had been granted, and that he met in the river, bund up, 7 schooners and a sloop, and out side of the bar, three more schooners, all from St. Jago (Cuba) with about 1,200 French passengers. A ship had also sailed from St. Jago with 500 passengers, bound to New-Orleans. *The True Republican or American Whig* [Vol. 1. No. 27] Wilmington, NC, Tuesday, 4 July 1809, page 3, column 3.

316. The ship Virginia was boarded by an officer from a British 74, who *impressed three seamen!!* Thus it goes, while Britain is talking of "friendly intercourse," her conduct evinces the most hostile intentions. Judge her, not by her words, but by her *actions*. *The True Republican or American Whig* [Vol. 1. No. 27] Wilmington, NC, Tuesday, 4 July 1809, page 3, column 4.

317. MARRIED, In this town on Tuesday evening last [27 June 1809], Mr. ***SAMUEL R. JOCELYN***, merchant, to Miss ***MARY ANN SAMPSON***, daughter of **Michael Sampson**, Esq. of Sampson County. *The True Republican or American Whig* [Vol. 1. No. 27] Wilmington, NC, Tuesday, 4 July 1809, page 3, column 4.

318. PORT OF WILMINGTON. *ENTERED*, Sloop Rover, **Philips**, Newport. Sch'r Eagle, **Sikes**, New-River. Sch'r Rover, **Whitby**, New-River. Sch'r Return, **Garret**, New-River. Sch'r Little John, **Capps**, New-River. Sch'r Resolution, **Fourman**, Swansborough. Sch'r Harmony, **Luce**, Philadelphia. Sch'r Jefferson, **Hall**, Boston. Brig Equator, **Ingersoll**, Boston. Sch'r Temperence, **Wellman**, Salem. Sch'r Amanda, **Magrath**, New-York. Brig Sterling, **Whitemarsh**, New-York. Sch'r Rising Sun, **Donnelly**, Philadelphia. Sch'r Sunbury, **Trippe**, Boston. Sch'r President, **Trippe**, Newport. Sloop Columbia, **Thompson**, Philadelphia. *CLEARED*. Sloop Betsy, **Pearce**, Kingston, (Jam.) Brig Iris, **Smith**, Charleston. Sch'r Dover, **Greene**, Boston. *The True Republican or American Whig* [Vol. 1. No. 27] Wilmington, NC, Tuesday, 4 July 1809, page 3, column 4.

319. *TO THE DEBTORS OF JOHN ECCLES*, Under the late Administration of **THOMAS ARCHIBALD** at Wilmington, *THIS NOTICE IS GIVEN*, THE Subscriber has twice noticed the said Debtors, and is sorry to say, without effect; *this is FINAL* and *without DISCRIMINATION*. Those Debtors that please to avail themselves of confessing Judgments, agreeably to former publications, can do so until this first of August, after that date Mr. **Jocelyn** will issue writs *indiscriminately*. **JOHN LORD**, Attorney, &c. N. B. Those who have made partial payments are

accepted. July 3. (ewtA.) *The True Republican or American Whig* [Vol. 1. No. 27] Wilmington, NC, Tuesday, 4 July 1809, page 3, column 4.

320. TAKE NOTICE. THE purchasers of Lots in the environs of Smithville, are earnestly requested to make payment previous to the 10th of August next, otherwise suits will be commenced against delinquents indiscriminately. **JOHN CONYERS**, and **SAMUEL POTTER**. *Commissioners. SMITHVILLE, July 1. The True Republican or American Whig* [Vol. 1. No. 27] Wilmington, NC, Tuesday, 4 July 1809, page 3, column 4.

321. TEN DOLLARS REWARD. *Ran away from the Subscriber*, ON the 7th instant, a Negro Fellow by the name of **CAESAR**, about thirty years of age, speaks slow, and one of his hands has been burnt when he was small, which had deformed it; he has also a hole in the crown of his hat. He was formerly the property of **M. M'Clammy**, deceased. I expect he will lurk about Wilmington or the Fort in Brunswick County, as he has acquaintances in both places; he may perhaps, on particularly occasions, lurk about Mr. **William Hansley**'s as he has a wife there. Whoever will deliver the said Negro to the Subscriber, on Topsail-Sound, or lodge him in the Wilmington jail, shall receive the above reward. N. B. Masters of vessels, and all other persons, are hereby forbid harboring, employing or carrying away said Negro, under the penalty of the law. **STOCKLEY SIDBURY**, jun. June 27. (tf.) *The True Republican or American Whig* [Vol. 1. No. 27] Wilmington, NC, Tuesday, 4 July 1809, page 3, column 4.

322. *DISSOLUTION of CO-PARTNERSHIP*. THE Co-partnership of *HALL & NICHOLS*, is this day dissolved, by mutual consent: All persons indebted to, & those who have claims against said FIRM, are requested to call on **C. Nichols**, for settlement, in his absence to apply to **J. Hall**. **JOHN HALL, CALEB NICHOLS**. *June 26*. (tf..) *The True Republican or American Whig* [Vol. 1. No. 27] Wilmington, NC, Tuesday, 4 July 1809, page 3, column 4.

323. *From Bell's (London) Messenger*. **AARON BURR**, AND [**Francisco**] **MIRANDA**. The Spanish Junta ambassador at London, (**Apadoca**) having made representations to the British minister for foreign affairs, that several persons were in London who had a hand in enterprise against the Spanish colonies in America, **Miranda** and **Burr** were particularly named, the former however, contrived to obtain a passage in a vessel bound to St. Christopher's, for which place it is said he departed: **Aaron Burr**, who was also summoned to appear, did not make his escape, but presented himself according to the summons, and was notified that he must depart from England; he disclaimed all connection or participation with any design against the Spanish colonies, and claimed as a British subject, under *magna charta*, to remain unmolested in the country, to which he owed and avowed allegiance! . . . He was nevertheless advised that he must depart the realm. . . he was accompanied to one of the ports on the North Sea, and shipt for the continent. We heard several weeks ago that he had taken his passage for the island of St. Christopher's, and was destined for Trinidad. *The True Republican or American Whig* [Vol. 1. No. 27] Wilmington, NC, Tuesday, 4 July 1809, page 4, column 2.

324. NOTICE. The Subscriber intends leaving the State during the summer and requests all those to whom he is indebted to call and receive payment. Those indebted will please pay these respective accounts to Mr. **A. L. Gomez**, who is fully authorized to settle all claims. **JACOB LEVY**. June 10. *The True Republican or American Whig* [Vol. 1. No. 27] Wilmington, NC, Tuesday, 4 July 1809, page 4, column 4.

325. PUBLISHED BY *THOMAS WATSON*, ON SECOND NEAR MARKET STREET. Three Dollars per annum, in advance, or three Dollars and fifty Cents, if not paid within the year. *The True Republican or American Whig* [Vol. 1. No. 45] Wilmington, NC, Tuesday, 7 November 1809, page 1, column 1.

326. *From the National Intelligencer.* THE NEW WORLD. No. IV. *An enquiry into the National Character of the people of the United States of America.* . . COLUMBIANUS. *The True Republican or American Whig* [Vol. 1. No. 45] Wilmington, NC, Tuesday, 7 November 1809, page 1, columns 1 -3.

327. COBBETT'S LETTER TO THE KING, *On the Maritime War against France.* Letter I. . . *The True Republican or American Whig* [Vol. 1. No. 45] Wilmington, NC, Tuesday, 7 November 1809, page 1, column 3 - page2, column 3.

328. *Philadelphia, Oct.* 19, 1809. We have been favored with the following extracts of letters, which exhibit in colors of to much truth, the deplorable condition of American commerce. *Copenhagen, July* 4. The American consul here has asked the government whether the relations between the U. States were friendly or not. They have answered they were friendly. He has also asked whether vessels bound to Sweden had been boarded by English cruisers, would be condemned according to present existing laws in Denmark, and they have answered they could not be condemned. . . There are now to the number of 25 American vessels in Norway and they are every day bringing in more. I think it worthy the serious consideration of government, whether they will suffer this property to be condemned. . . *The True Republican or American Whig* [Vol. 1. No. 45] Wilmington, NC, Tuesday, 7 November 1809, page 2, column 4 & page 3, column 1.

329. WILMINGTON, TUESDAY, NOVEMBER 7, 1809. The Legislature of this State will meet on Monday the 20th instant, and Congress will meet on the Monday following. The Federal Circuit Court will commence at Raleigh, on Monday the 13th instant. *The True Republican or American Whig* [Vol. 1. No. 45] Wilmington, NC, Tuesday, 7 November 1809, page 3, column 1.

330. The collector of the port of New-York has received instructions to clear out vessels for any of the Spanish ports in the Bay of Biscay, although the troops of Ferdinand VII or Napoleon Bonaparte may be in possession thereth. *The True Republican or American Whig* [Vol. 1. No. 45] Wilmington, NC, Tuesday, 7 November 1809, page 3, column 2.

331. Brigadier General **WADE HAMPTON**, passed through Augusta (Geo.) on the 7th inst., on his way to Natchez, in the vicinity of which place, it is understood, about 1000 regular troops are stationed. This departure of General **Hampton** for Head-Quarters seems to strengthen the report of *Wilkinson's recall*. *The True Republican or American Whig* [Vol. 1. No. 45] Wilmington, NC, Tuesday, 7 November 1809, page 3, column 2.

332. The General Assembly of Connecticut has appointed his Excellency **John Treadwell**, Governor of that state, in the room of his Excellency Governor **Jonathan Trumbull**, deceased. *The True Republican or American Whig* [Vol. 1. No. 45] Wilmington, NC, Tuesday, 7 November 1809, page 3, column 2.

333. A bill has been introduced into the legislature of Tennessee, now in session, prohibiting the drawing of all private Lotteries. *The True Republican or American Whig* [Vol. 1. No. 45] Wilmington, NC, Tuesday, 7 November 1809, page 3, column 2.

334. *Boston, Oct.* 24. Yesterday the brig Joseph, Capt. **Fostester**, arrived at this port, in 53 days from Malaga; bringing the Malaga Diary to the 19th Sept. Captain **F.**, states the best informed in Malaga were extremely anxious for the fate of their country and themselves; considering their case as hopeless, If Austria made peace, which was expressed. The paper of the 19th September states that the divisions of Marshal Ney and Soult had separated. The former had proceeded towards Salamanca. Soult's army occupied the highlands of Estremadura; his headquarters were at Placenta. *The True Republican or American Whig* [Vol. 1. No. 45] Wilmington, NC, Tuesday, 7 November 1809, page 3, column 2.

335. The United States brig NAUTILUS, commanded by Lieut. **Arthur Sinclair**, on the 19th ult., weighed anchor and proceeded from Washington on a cruise off the coast. *The True Republican or American Whig* [Vol. 1. No. 45] Wilmington, NC, Tuesday, 7 November 1809, page 3, column 3.

336. PORT OF WILMINGTON. *ENTERED*, Sch'r Three Brothers, **Atwood**, Charleston. Sch'r Rising Sun, **Chase**, New-York. Sch'r Adams, **Eldridge**, Boston. Sch'r Traveller, **Atwood**, Barnstable. Sch'r Julia & Sally, **Starr**, New-York. Brig Neptune, **Curtis**, Grenada. *CLEARED*, Sch'r Lydia, ------, Boston. Sch'r Sally, **Hicks**, Philadelphia. Brig Joshua Potts, **Magrath**, Philadelphia. Sch'r Traveller, **Atwood**, Boston. *The True Republican or American Whig* [Vol. 1. No. 45] Wilmington, NC, Tuesday, 7 November 1809, page 3, column 3.

337. TOWN LOTS. FOR SALE by the subscriber, the following lots, some of which have buildings and other improvements thereon, viz. One Lot at the north part of the town, known by the name of the Still House Lot, having a dwelling house, tar-shed and wharf thereon. Four Lots in front of the subscriber's dwelling house, viz. No. 1, at the corner of Third and Orange streets, with the Windmill, which will be sold separately or together, as may suit the purchasers. No. 2, on Orange Street, with a well finished dwelling house and suitable outbuildings on the same. No. 3, a vacant Lot. No. 4, on the corner of Orange and Fourth streets, with buildings. Lots B. No. 119 and 114, vacant. If the above Lots are not sold before the expiration of the present month, they will be put at public auction, of which due notice will be given. **R. LANGDON**. Nov. 6. 3w. *The True Republican or American Whig* [Vol. 1. No. 45] Wilmington, NC, Tuesday, 7 November 1809, page 3, column 3.

338. AT A MEETING *Of the Commissioners of the Town, November 2d,* 1809. THE driving of Horse through the streets to water, or other purposes, being productive of danger to the inhabitants, especially to children. *Ordered* that after Friday next, the 10th instant, no Horse or Horse be driven loose through the street, but that all Horses be ridden or led by bridles or halters, under penalty for each and every offence against this ordinance, forty shillings if committed by a free person, or fifteen lashes of the whipping post, if by a slave. **TH: CALLENDER**, *T. Clerk*. *The True Republican or American Whig* [Vol. 1. No. 45] Wilmington, NC, Tuesday, 7 November 1809, page 3, column 3.

339. RANAWAY FROM the subscriber, on the 15th September last, a Negro Fellow named **HARRY**, about five feet eight inches high, stout built, coarse complexion, large teeth in the fore part of his mouth, and plausible in his conversation. A liberal reward will be given to whoever will deliver the said Negro to the subscriber in Wilmington, or lodge him in some jail where he may be got. **JAMES USHER**. Oct. 31. tf. *The True Republican or American Whig* [Vol. 1. No. 45] Wilmington, NC, Tuesday, 7 November 1809, page 3, column 3.

340. NOTICE. CIRCUMSTANCES rendering it inconvenient for the subscriber to leave this State agreeably to his former intentions, he begs leave to inform his customers and the public general, that he continues to carry on the business of his profession as a Tailor in its various branches. He trusts from his experience, to give satisfaction to those who may favor him with their custom at his old stand in Market-Street, a few doors east of Messrs. Geer & Avery's corner store. **J. MACCOLL**. Oct. 17. 3w. *The True Republican or American Whig* [Vol. 1. No. 45] Wilmington, NC, Tuesday, 7 November 1809, page 3, column 4.

341. MISS **BEZE**, FROM New-York, WHICH place she left on account of her health, has the honor of informing the Ladies and Gentlemen of Wilmington, and of the Carolinas, that she will open in Wilmington, a School for teaching Music, French, Drawing and Needle Work. Lesson will be given every day, except Saturdays, on the following terms: *per month, Entrance*. Music & Piano Forte $6 $4, French Language $4 $8, Drawing and Painting $4 $3, Needle Work $3 $3. As Miss **B**'s house is large, airy and convenient, being situated on the top of the hill in Dock Street,

in a healthy situation and as her parents live with her, young ladies can be accommodated with board. To them will be taught, if necessary, Reading, Writing, Arithmetic and Geography. The School will be opened on the first of September next. Young ladies will be taught in the morning and gentlemen in the afternoon. Miss **B**'s drawings and paintings can be seen at her house, as well as several letters of the parents whose children have been taught by her, expressing that satisfaction of her tuition, and their regret at her departure. Miss **B** will take likenesses in miniature. August 25. *The True Republican or American Whig* [Vol. 1. No. 45] Wilmington, NC, Tuesday, 7 November 1809, page 3, column 4.

342. NEW STORE. The Subscribers have just received by the schooner Venus from New York, and are now offering at the store formerly occupied by Lloyd & Anderson, a general assortment of DRY GOODS and GROCERIES which they offer for sale at reduced prices for cash or country produce. They have on hand a few elegant copies of Brown's Family Bible. **DAVID & RICHARD LLOYD**. Sept. 18. 3w. *The True Republican or American Whig* [Vol. 1. No. 45] Wilmington, NC, Tuesday, 7 November 1809, page 3, column 4.

343. Fayetteville Academy. THE Trustees of the Fayetteville Academy, with pleasure inform the parents and guardians of children that the Rev. **WM. L. TURNER**[36] is engaged as Principal Teacher in the Seminary, and will enter upon the duties of his appointment about the middle of November next. The degree of reputation this gentleman has deserved and enjoyed as Principal of the Academy in Raleigh, renders unnecessary the addition of anything on this head. It forms a sure pledge to those who purpose placing their children at this school that the utmost attention will be paid to their advancement in literature and the improvement of their morals. The Trustees assure the public that nothing shall be wanting on their part to promote the future usefulness of the students that depend on a steady discharge of their trust. They contemplate, and have partly arranged an enlarged plan of education in the Female Department, and the addition of a Teacher in Music. The convenience of the Students as respects board, has engaged the particular attention of the Trustees. Accommodations for a large number of each sex in the principal families of the town, may be had at the rate of six or seven dollars per month. The central situation of Fayetteville; the very ready communication with all parts of the state, the degree of health enjoyed by its inhabitants, joined to the known and approved abilities of the Teachers renders the Fayetteville Academy highly deserving of public notice and patronage. **D. ANDERSON**, *Pres't*. Sept. 30. 6w. *The True Republican or American Whig* [Vol. 1. No. 45] Wilmington, NC, Tuesday, 7 November 1809, page 4, column 3.

344. FOR SALE, *The HOUSE and LOT* At present occupied by Doctor **Daniel M'Neill. GEO. W. B. BURGWIN**. Aug. 28. tf. *The True Republican or American Whig* [Vol. 1. No. 45] Wilmington, NC, Tuesday, 7 November 1809, page 4, column 3.

---

[36] The Rev. **William Leftwich Turner** was born in Virginia in 1773. He was the fourth pastor of the First Presbyterian Church in Fayetteville, North Carolina. He was called to serve in 1809 and came there from Raleigh. He died on 18 October 1813. His remains were interred in Cross Creek Cemetery, Block 19, in Fayetteville. Turner's will was probated in December 1813 in Cumberland County, Book A, page 199. The Fayetteville Academy was in place of the Fayetteville Seminary, chartered 1799. The Rev. Turner was placed in charge of the Academy in 1809 and remained there until his death. The Academy burned down in 1831 and the lot was sold to private parties. Thanks to the Rev. A. L. Phillips, *An Historical Sketch of the Presbyterian Church of Fayetteville, N.C.* (1889) page 14, and to John A. Oates, *The Story of Fayetteville and the Upper Cape Fear* (1981) page 450. Also thanks to Anna S. Sherman, *Cross Creek Cemetery Number One, Cumberland County, Fayetteville, North Carolina* (1988) and to Kate J. Lepine, *Will Abstracts, Cumberland County, North Carolina, 1754-1863* (1983).

345. LIST OF LETTERS *Remaining in the Wilmington Post Office, October 1st*, 1809. Major **Sam'l Ashe**, N. Hanover County, 2; **John Allen**, 2; **William Atkins, Thomas Archibald, J. Atterbury.**

B. **John Barrett**, New-Hanover County, **Susannah Baldwin**, Brunswick Co., 2. **Wm. Boyd**, do. Dr. **Benjamin Ballard, James Brian, N. Brown, Asa Brooks, Sam'l Barlow**, Miss **Beze, James Byrns, Sarah Barlow, Thomas Bishop, William Barret, Wm. Boatright, Chester Barrows, Ephraim Brete, William Blumpe.**

C. **Hugh G. Campbell, Robert Carmott, John Conyers**, 2; Clerk of the Superior Court, Brunswick County, **Charles Carrol**, Bladen County, **Daniel Chisholm, Charles Conell**, Mrs. **Harriot, Ann Cummins, Rob't Wm. Crooksbanks**, 2; **James Corbett, Richard Cheese, Benjamin Cooper, John Cowan, James Collier, Alex'r Cox, Henry Crafford, Wm. Collins, Thos. Caslin, Rowland Craig**, Capt. **John Clarke**, jun.

D. Mrs. **Ann Dickson**, N. Hanover County, **Thomas Davis, Wm. Davis, John Davis, Wilson Davis, Joseph Davis, W-ty. Davis, John Dunlap**, Brunswick, **Nicholas Darrel, John Dickey**, 3; Donaldson, McMillan & Co. **R. Duplainy, Terrin Derremier.**

E. **Jonathan Elwell.**

F. **Thos. Fitzgerald**, Mrs. **E. Fleming, Thos. Flowers**, 2.

G. **Wm. I. Graining, David Greer**, Capt. **A. Golden, Mathew Gleason, Thos. Griffiths, Lewis Goff, Jacob Golden, David Gellespie.**

H. Messrs. **W. & A. Hattridge**, Mrs. **Hooper**, 2; Capt. **Wm. Hall**, Capt. **John Hall**, Mrs. **Ann Holmes, Alex. Hines**, Messrs. Hooper & Mitchell, **Isabelle Hartman**, Mr. **Donald Henderson**, Cumberland County; **Chas. Hardy, John Harris, Thos. Howard**, 6; **Bartlett Holmes, Sam'l. Hall**, Brunswick County; Messrs. **J. Cowan, M. Hill & J. Hartman**, Mr. **William Henry, Christ. Georgeton Hatter**; **John Howard, Robert Howe**, Mrs. **Margaret Howe, Jas. Huse, Francis Henry, Judith Halsing, Peggy Halling, Saml. K. Hodges.**

J. **Cedk. Jones, George Jones, Benj. Jacobs, Penelope Johnston.**

L. Mrs. **Sarah A. Lillington**, Mrs. **Jane Lanestead**, 2; **J. M. Lewis, Wm. Lee, Sam'l. Livingston, Wm. Larkin, Wm. Lishman**, 3; **Laspycress, Ezekiel Lane.**

M. Mrs. **S. Mosely**, Major **A. D. Moore, George M'Kenzie, Roger Moore, John M'Auslan, Henry Myrover, Hugh Murphie, Thomas Mabson, John M'Dougald, John M'Lenning, Peter M'Bryde, John M'Kenzie**, Capt. **Newberry Moore, Benj. Mills**, Brunswick County, Capt. **Allen M'Lean, John M'Allester, Thomas M'Connell, Donald M'Leod, Peggy Mooter, H. Merec.**

N. Miss **E. Nutt**, Clerk of the District Court, **Richmond Nolly**, 2; **Rueben Newton**, 2; **Richard Nixon, Job Neal**, Sheriff of New Hanover County, Dr. **Josiah Nash.**

O. **Dan'l O'Neal**, Capt. **J. S. Oliver**, 2.

P. **C. & P. Pelham**, 7; **Hector Paine**, Mrs. **E. Price, James Price, John Pollock, Lewis Pollock, B. Perkins**, 6; **Amos Perry**, Brunswick County.

R. Capt. **Matthias Rich**, 2; **N. W. Ruggles**, 5; **John Robeson**, Capt. **Geo. Rhodes, Wm. Roberds, John P. Redbrook, Wm. B. Redman, L. Ramsey, Thos. Russ.**

S. Mrs. **L. M. Swift, John Scott**, 3; Capt. **H. Smith**, jun. Capt. **R. Scott**, Mrs. **Lydia Sullivan, John Smith, Tabitha Simpson**, Capt. **Z. Swain, James Smith**, Major **John Scull, Thomas Snead, Henry Sampson, Jonathan Stanley.**

T. **David Tuman, Arthur Tyler**, Capt. **John Taylor.**

W. **Carleton Walker, Christopher Wallace, John A. Watson**, Messrs. **John Wilkings & Co.** Mr. **Wm. A. Wilkings**, Mr. **Wm. Williams, Henry Watters, Eleazer Watterman, John Waddle, Wm. Wilkes**, 2; Mrs. **Margaret Walker, Robt. Williams**, Capt. **Thos. Wiley.**

V. **Wm. H. Van**, Madame **Veragan**. *The True Republican or American Whig* [Vol. 1. No. 45] Wilmington, NC, Tuesday, 7 November 1809, page 4, column 4.

346. A SCHOOL WILL be commenced by the Subscriber on Monday 30th inst. In the Hall in the Dwelling House of Mrs. **Kenan** in Wilmington. *The Terms will be*, For Geography, Navigation, Surveying & the various branches of the Mathematics, per quarter, $6. Arithmetic & English Grammar $5. Reading and Writing $4. Spelling &c. $3. Every attention will be paid to the manners and morals of Pupils. The favor and patronage of Gentlemen, Parents & Guardians in Wilmington, and its vicinity, will be greatly acknowledged by **AMOS WHEELER**, *Jun*. The Subscriber will also commence an *Evening School* at the same place on the 6th in November next, in which the above branches will be taught. For further particulars enquire at Mrs. **Dorsey**'s, Oct. 23. *The True Republican or American Whig* [Vol. 1. No. 45] Wilmington, NC, Tuesday, 7 November 1809, page 4, column 4.

347. Know all men by these presents that I **John Ramsey** of Wilmington in the County of New Hanover State of North Carolina for & in consideration of the term of Twelve hundred dollars to me in hand paid by **Thomas Watson** of Newbern in the State aforesaid Printers, the receipt whereof I do hereby acknowledge have granted bargained sold and delivered and by these presents do grant bargain sell and deliver unto the said **Thomas Watson** the whole of the Types printing Material and all the apparatus contained in the printing office of the True Republican or American Whig at Wilmington, North Carolina to wit, one Printing press, one fount of Long primer, one ditto of small Pica, one ditto of English, one ditto of pica, one ditto of Script, and a quantity of frames, composing Sticks, chesses, Boards & c, and together therewith the whole of my interest in and to any & every parts of the Estate of my said father **Matthew Ramsey**, late of the County of Chatham, deceased. . . In and shall well and duly pay unto the said **Thomas Watson** . . . the sum of four hundred dollars in twelve months and a further sum of four hundred dollars in eighteen months, from the Sixth day of November One thousand Eight hundred and nine with interest from the date on each of said sums, according to the terms of three promissory notes of that date . . . and this hereby declared to be the intention of the parties hereto that he the said **John Ramsey** is to retain in his possession the whole of the aforegranted and bargained premises in order to enable him to raise the money to be paid. . . In Witness where of I have hereunto set my hand & seal this fourth day of January Eighteen hundred and ten. **John Ramsey** New Hanover County Deed Book N, pages 532 and 533. Thank you Dr. A. B. Pruitt, *Abstracts of Deeds New Hanover Co, NC Books N & O* (2006).

348. State of North Carolina, Wilmington ~ Received from **John Ramsey** a Bill of sale of all the Types and printing apparatus belonging to the office of the True Republican as well as every other species of property, . . and discharge the said **John Ramsey** of any rights, claims or demand which I might had had by virtue of the wither Mortgage, And I do further agree to pay and discharge all the debts contracted by the said **John Ramsey** on account of the firm of **Watson & Ramsey**, and I do further agree to pay the house rent & Negro hire which were necessary in carrying out the printing business in the said office, since the dissolution of the Copartnership up to February 9th, 1810. **Th. Watson**. New Hanover County Deed Book N, page 537. Thanks to Dr. Pruitt.

349. DIED. In this city, on Sunday night last, Mr. **John Ramsey**, a native of Chatham County, but for several years past a resident of Wilmington. *Raleigh Register*, Tuesday, 15 November 1825, page 3. Thank you to Lois S. Neal, *Abstracts of Vital Records from Raleigh, NC Newspapers 1820-1829* (1980).

The True Republican or American Whig 1809
By Joseph E. Waters Sheppard

NAMES INDEX

Adams, John (page 1), 156, 225, 288
Addison, Judge 108
Allen 012, 303
Allen, John 345
Alston, Thomas H. 094
Ancrum, James H. 126
Anderson 289
Anderson, D. 343
Anderson, David 008
Anthony, Stephen 169
Archibald, Thomas 319, 345
Armistead, Addison B. 175
Armory, Thomas C. 040
Armstrong, Gen. 105
Ashe, Samuel 091, 169, 247, 345
Atkins, William 169, 345
Atterbury, J. 345
Atwood 336 (3)

Backius 202
Bailard, Susanna 153
Bailey 012
Ballard, Benjamin 169, 345
Baker 073
Baker, Joshua L. 169
Baldwin, Susannah 345
Bales, Thomas 292
Baly, Christopher 292
Barker, Gen. 076
Barkman 012, 088, 202
Barkman, John 222
Barlow, Sam'l 345
Barlow, Sarah 345
Barret, William 345
Barrett, John 345
Barrows, Chester 345
Barton 183
Basset, Mr. 050
Bates 224
Beard, David 299
Beasley, John 169
Beats 183
Beatty, Thomas J. 032, 039
Beck, Elizabeth 133
Befunt, John 169
Beggs, James 171
Beitner, Eliza 154
Belanger, Mr. 091, 130
Belanger, F. J. 176
Bell, Thomas 215
Bellugs, Stephen 169
Bellune, Daniel 169
Benjamin, P. 143
Bernard 289
Berry, William Graves 126
Beze, Miss 341, 345
Bishop, Thos. 169, 345
Bittall 104
Bloodworth, William 169
Bludworth, Lewis 214

Bludworth, Sam'l 211
Bludworth, Thomas 214
Blumpe, William 345
Boatright, Wm. 345
Bob, runaway 291
Bonaparte, Eliza 234
Bonaparte, Napoleon 177, 287
Bonaparte, Napoleon Louis 234
Bostwick 104
Bourne 012
Bourne, George 252
Bowen 224
Bowman 183, 224
Boyd, Wm. 345
Bradey, Joshua 140 (2)
Bradford, Capt. 218
Bradley, John 008
Bradly, Francis 292
Brass, Andrew 292
Braston 289
Brete, Ephraim 345
Brian, James 345
Brooks, Asa 345
Brown 224
Brown, G. 169
Brown, John 013
Brown, John C. 169
Brown, Joshua 086
Brown, N. 345
Brown, Robert W. 196, 274, 283, 285
Bryant, Austen 114
Bryant, Cyrus 169
Buckhannon, Jeremiah 169
Burgwin, George W. B. 019, 173, 344
Burgwin, John F. 048
Burgwin & Orme 168, 173, 253
Burr, Aaron (page 1), 309, 323 (2)
Burr, Capt. 299
Burwell, Mr. 028
Buxton, Frances 154
Byrns, James 345

Caesar, runaway 321
Caldwell, Joseph 160, 272
Callender, Thomas 058, 193, 338
Cameron 224
Cameron, Capt. 246
Cameron, George 257
Camack, Mr. 237
Camock, D. 111
Camock, R. 111
Campbell, G. W. 004
Campbell, Hugh 079, 345
Campbell, William 008
Canning, Mr. 060 (2), 061, 062, 063
Canning, George 061, 177
Canu, Mr. 185
Capps 289, 318
Carman 045
Carmott, Robert 345

The True Republican or American Whig 1809
By Joseph E. Waters Sheppard

Carolina, runaway 263
Carpenter, Peter 169
Carroll, Charles 169, 345
Cartwright 303 (2)
Caslin, Thos. 345
Chairis 303
de Champagny, 177
de Chanla, 195, 212
Charlton, Thomas 292
Chase 289, 303, 336
Cheese, Richard 345
Childs, T. 169
Chisholm, Daniel 345
Church, R. 169
Clark, F. 040
Clark, James 069
Clarke, John 192 (2), 345
Clarke, Jonah 169
Clements, T. 169
Clinton, George 052 (2)
Cochran, Robert 057, 192
Cohen, Philip 086
Collier, James 345
Collins 240
Collins, James 169
Collins, Wm. 345
Colvin, John 147
Conell, Charles 345
Connel, Capt. 038
Connelly, Capt. 152
Conway, Patrick 181
Conyers, John 194, 320, 345
Cooke, Henry M. 154
Cooper, Benjamin 345
Cooper, William 169
Corbett, James 345
Cotton, Adam 169
Cowan, I. 091
Cowan, J. 345
Cowan, John 345
Cowan, T. 131, 150
Cox, Alex'r 345
Cox, William 175
Crabtree 012, 045
Crafford, Henry 345
Craig, Rowland 345
Creighton, Eleanor 010
Crossbanks, Robert W. 345
Crutch, Richard 291
Cummins, Ann 345
Curtis 202, 336

Dana, Mr. 115
Dana, N. 304
Daniel, Stephen B. 169, 222
Darrell 073
Darrell, Nicholas 169, 345
Davidson 073
Davidson, Wm. 169
Davis 164, 224
Davis, John 345
Davis, Joseph 345

Davis, Thomas 345
Davis, Wm. 345
Davis, Wilson 345
Davis, W-ty 345
Davison, Mr. 169
Day, Thomas 169
Dearborn, Gen. 077
Decatur, Stephen 091
Delgairnes, Alex'r 169
Demar, runaway 247
Dennin 303
Denning 045
Dennison 073
DeRosset, A. J. 262
Derremier, Terrin 345
Dick, Mr. 091, 149
Dick, William 018, 238, 279
Dickey, John 345
Dickinson, Mr. 047
Dickson, Alexander 169
Dickson, Ann 345
Dickson, James 111
Donnelly 318
Dorsey, Mrs. 346
Dougherty, Patrick 108
Douglas, Capt. 041
Downing, Jas. 169
Drysdale 202
Dudley, Ann 103
Dudley, Capt. 091
Dudley, Christopher 103
Duffy, William 258
Dunbibin, Junius C. 066, 067, 306, 307
Duncan, george 169
Dundas, David 287
Dundas, Harry 271
Dunham 073
Dunlap, James 109
Dunlap, John 345
Dunn, Alexander 017
Dunn, Samuel 069
Dunn, Wm. 069
Dunner, Capt. 041
Duplainy, R. 345
Dyer, J. 169

Eccles, John 319
Eldridge 336
Eliza, child in deed *footnote* 18 (page 19)
Ellingwood, J. 169
Elwell, Jonathan 345
English, Charles 292
Eppe, Mr. 037, 312
Erskine, Mr. 159 92)
Eustis, William 241
Everitt, Reuben 068, 169

Ferdinand VII 191
Fitzgerald, Thos. 345
Fleming, E. 345
Fleming, I. 016, 044
Fleming, J. 189

The True Republican or American Whig 1809
By Joseph E. Waters Sheppard

Fleming, James 124
Flora, runaway 248
Flowers, Thos. 345
Foote, John 249
Forster, Mr. 284
Fostester, Capt. 334
Fourman 318
Foy, Frederick 311
Franklin, Edward 169
Freeman, John 169

Gardane, M. 251
Gardenier, Mr. 037
Garnier, John 084
Garrett 289 (2), 318
Garrot 073
Gaston, Mr. 240
Gauiter & Co. 032, 039, 236
Gautier, Capt. 091 (2)
Gautier, Thomas N. 013, 032, 040 (2), 216, 236, 246
Geers, Gilbert 080
Gellespie, David 345
George, runaway 258
Gibson, James T. 010
Giles, William 008, 122
Giles & Burgwin 031
Giles, William Branch 001, 026, 091
Gillespie, George 169
Gillett, Benjamin C. 033
Given, John 170
Glassen, Geo. 169
Gleason, Mathew 345
Goff, Lewis 345
Golden, Capt. A. 345
Golden, Jacob 345
Gomez 164
Gomaz, A. L. 324
Gomez, Aaron 169
Goodrich, Mr. 003
Goodvine 104, 164
Goulden, J. 169
Grafton 289
Graining, Wm. I. 345
Grandy, Thomas 142
Grange, John 263
Grant 303
Green, John 262
Greene 318
Greer, David 345
Griffin 202 (2)
Griffiths, Thos. 345
Guyteer, Nathaniel 169

Hadnot, William 311
Hailey 164
Hall 245 (2), 289, 303, 318
Hall, Capt. 053
Hall, A. 169
Hall, Allmand *footnote* 16 (page 17), 276, 311
Hall, Benj. 169
Hall, Elizabeth 132
Hall, John 132, 322, 345

Hall, Salmon (page 1), 021, 024, 036
Hall, Sam'l 345
Hall, William 169, 345
Halling, Peggy 345
Halling, Solomon 030, 079, 244
Hallowell 045
Halsey, Wm. H. *footnote* 10 (page 7)
Halsing, Judith 345
Hampton, Brig. Gen. Wade 331
Handy, William S. 169
Hannahan, Mr. 169
Hannis, Sarah Graves 223
Hansley, William 321
Hardy, Chas. 345
Harkin 045
Harrington, Henry W. 162
Harriot, Mrs. 345
Harris, John 345
Harris, William 169
Harrison, William Henry 243
Harry, runaway 263, 339
Hartman, Isabelle 345
Hartman, Jacob 115, 345
Hasell, William Soranzo (page 1), (page 2), 025, 043,
    065, 116, 120, 145, 266, 275, 277, 290
Hatch, Edward 213
Hatter, Christ. Georgeton 345
Hattridge, A. 345
Hattridge, Wm. 117, 345
Haws 183
Hegrose, John 169
Henderson, Donald 345
Henderson, J. M. 125
Henry, Francis 345
Henry, William 345
Heron, Alice 127
Hewson, Hugh 293
Hicks 336
Hill, Heny 071
Hill, John 013
Hill, M. 345
Hill, N. 125
Hill, William 103, 237
Hill, William H. 261
Hillhouse, Mr. 026, 059
Hines, Alex. 345
Hinson, John 175
Hitch 088
Hobbs, J. E. 286
Hobbs, Mr. 150
Hodges, P. 169, 237
Hodges, Samuel K. 345
Hogg, John 007
Holmes 012, 202, 224
Holmes, Ann 345
Holmes, Bartlett 345
Holmes, James 154
Hooper, George 008
Hooper, Mrs. 345
Hopkins 073, 104
Hopton, Abner 169
Houston, John 080

The True Republican or American Whig 1809
By Joseph E. Waters Sheppard

Howard, Elie 169
Howard, John 345
Howard, Thos. 345
Howe, Miss 311
Howe, Margaret 345
Howe, Robert 169, 345
Howell, Mr. 150
Hubbel, William 169
Huggins, Cooper 311
Hull 289
Hunter, Capt. 110
Hunter, Thomas 249, 280
Hurst, Cornelius 169
Huse, James 169, 345

Ingersoll 224, 245, 318
Ireson 224, 245

Jack, runaway 085, 171
Jackson, J. G. 155
Jacob, runaway 140
Jacob, Benjamin 215, 345
Jacobs, Joseph 169
James, Mary 154
Jarvis 104, 164, 183, 289
Jefferson, Thomas (page 1), 060, 146, 252, 267
Jeffrey, John 118
Jenkins 183, 202, 289
Jennett, Jesse 195, 212, 284
Jennings, Thomas 118
Jessa, runaway 280
Jocelyn, Mr. 319
Jocelyn, Samuel R. 317
John, runaway 213
John VI 071
Johnson, Jeremiah 169
Johnson, Nancy 169
Johnson, Tarleton 094
Johnston, Penelope 345
Jones 202
Jones, Cedk. 345
Jones, David 308
Jones, Felix 191
Jones, George 345
Jones, J. C. 053
Jones, Jacques 169
Jones, Rice 109
Jones, Robert Hill 192 (2), 240
Jones, William 076, 147, 248
Jones, William W. 169
Joyce 012 (2)
Judge, Israel 114
Junot, Andoche *footnote* 17 (page 18)
Jupitor or Jube 311

Kamir, Count 138
Kelly, H. 009, 110, 202
Kelly, Hanson 010, 126, 174, 313
Kenan, Daniel L. 154
Kenan, Mrs. 346
Kenan, Owen 083, 085
Kenan, Thos. 091

Kennedy 104, 224
Key, Philip B. 042
King, Rufus 052
Klevenhausen, Herman 169
Klopstock, F. G. 030

Lafavour 245
Lake, Capt. 315
Lane, Ezekiel 169, 345
Lanestead, Jane 345
Langdon, John 052
Langdon, R. 337
Larkin, Wm. 345
Larkins, T. 171
Larkins, William Jones 147
Laspycress 345
Latham, Daniel 086
Law, John 169
Lazarus, A. 113, 120, 305
Lazarus, Aaron 008
Lee, Maclin 169
Lee, Wm. 345
Lefavour 289
Lefton, Nathan B. 169
Leib, J. 076
Leonard, Jacob W. 048, 049, 139, 167, 184, 228
Lesters, Jeremiah 169
Levy, Jacob 111, 245, 324
Lewis 245 (2)
Lewis, Gov. 243
Lewis, J. M. 345
Lillington, Sarah A. 345
Lincoln, Levi 075
Lishman, Wm. 345
Littlejohn, Wm. 055
Livingston 012, 104
Livingston, Betsy 169
Livingston, Sam'l. 345
Lloyd, David 342
Lloyd, Edward 301
Lloyd, Richard 342
London, John 008, 115
Lord, J. 169
Lord, John 319
Lowry, Robert 169
Lucas, Mr. 264
Lucas, Richard 278
Luce 318
Lucy, runaway 127
Luke, runaway 291
Lyman, Erastus 156

MacAuslan, John 117, 345
MacColl, John 239, 340
MacNeill, A. F. 014, 020, 091
McAllester, John 345
McBryde, Peter 345
McCall, Mr. 091
McClammy, M. 321
McCole, Catharine 169
McCole, John 169
McConnell, Thomas 345

73

The True Republican or American Whig 1809
By Joseph E. Waters Sheppard

McDougald, John 345
McIlhenny 073, 104 (2), 164, 202, 245, 289 (2), 303 (2)
McKay, D. 188
McKean, Thomas 023
McKeel, William 169
McKenzie, George 345
McKenzie, John 345
McKenzie, William *footnote* 34 (page 51)
McLachlan, Capt. *footnote* 17 (page 18)
McLean 045 (2), 073, 088, 164, 303
McLean, Allen 345
McLearan, Duncan 008
McLenning, John 345
McLeod, Capt. 292
McLeod, Donald 345
McLin, Thomas 154
McMillan, John 008
McMullin, Robert 076
McNeill, Dr. Daniel 344
McRae, Duncan 258
Mabson, Thomas 244, 345
Madison, James (page 1), 052 (2), 060, 062, 083, 091, 105, 107, 269
Madison, John 163
Magrath, Capt. 313, 318, 336
Malbourne, Francis 298, 302
Mallet, Daniel 280
Mallett, Henrietta Ann 079
Mallett, Peter 079
Manning, Moses 082
Maria I *footnote* 17 (page 18)
Marino de Sevilla, Fr. 191
Marshall, Mrs. 169
Martin, John 123, 255
Mason, John 219
Maxwell, Peter 257
Mayden 289
Meares, James 171
Merec, H. 345
Merrick, George 311
Miller, Jas. 169
Miller, William 169
Mills, Benj. 345
Minot, Henry 169
Minotti 289
Miranda, Francisco 323
Mitchell, John 258
Mitchell, Robert 008, 247
Mitchell, William 247
Molly, theft 142
Monnino, Joseph 186
Monpoey, Honore 086 (2)
Monroe, James 052
Montgomery 202
Mooney, Geo. 170
Moore, Maj. A. D. 345
Moore, Elizabeth 244
Moore, Hillory 140
Moore, John 160
Moore, Sir John 206, 296
Moore, Judge 259

Moore, N. 141
Moore, Capt. Newberry 345
Moore, Roger 345
Moorhead, Thomas 292
Mooter, Peggy 345
Morgan, Alexander 169
Morrison, Capt. 178
Mosely, Mrs. S. 345
Mosely, Wm. 169
Moses, runaway 263
Mumford, Wm. B. 169
Murphie, Hugh 345
Musgroves, Mrs. 169
Muter, Margaret 011
Muter, Robert 011
Myrover, Henry 345

Nash, Dr. Josiah 345
Neal, Job 345
Nelson 164
Nelson, Mr. 029
Nettles, Capt. 169
Newton, Daniel 311
Newton, Mr. 050
Newton, James 169
Newton, Rueben 345
Nichols, Caleb 322
Nixon, Richard 169, 345
Noble, Samuel 171
Nolly, Richmond 345
Norman, Sarah 154
Nutt, Miss E. 345
Nutt, William 276

Oakley, Charles 159
Ogden, Col. 187
Oliver 073, 104
Oliver, J. S. 345
O'Neal, Dan'l. 345
Orme, James 173
Orme, Burgwin & 168, 173, 253
Osborne, Edwin J. 143
Owen 164, 181
Owens 202 (2), 289
Owens, Capt. 283

Paine, Hector 345
Parke, James 169
Patterson 200
Patterson, John 169
Pearce 303, 318
Pearson, William 292
Pearsons 183
Pee 139
Pelham, C. & P. 345
Pennicke, Solomon 169
Perkins, B. 345
Perret, Lewis 185
Perry, Amos 345
Petenson, Alexander 169
Peter, runaway 171, 262
Peyton, Dr. 055

The True Republican or American Whig 1809
By Joseph E. Waters Sheppard

Philips 318
Pickering, Mr. 059
Pickering, Timothy 076, 158
Pinckney, Mr. 060 (3), 061, 062, 063
Pinckney, Charles Cotesworth (page 1), 052, 150
Pinckney, William 060, 061, 062, 063
Pitkin, Mr. 312
Pollock, John 345
Pollock, Lewis 345
Porter, William 086
Potter, Henry 192, 240
Potter, Mr. 298
Potter, Samuel 320
Potter, Sylvia W. *footnote* 33 (page 50)
Potter, Washington 086
Potts, Joshua 091 (2)
Poutnap, William 169
Prevost, George 220
Price, Mrs. E. 345
Price, James 248, 345
Price, Wm. 169
Punchard 245
Purviance, Mr. 064

Quincy, Mr. 065 (2), 072

Ramsey, John (page 1), *footnote* 18 (page 19), 090, 096, 347, 348, 349
Ramsey, L. 345
Ramsey, Matthew 347
Randolph, Mr. 004, 105
Ravis, runaway 118
Redbrook, John P. 345
Reddings 289
Redman, Wm. B. 345
Redmond, James 169
Reinhold, Mrs. 169
Rhodes 088, 224, 289
Rhodes, Geo. 345
Rhodes, John Felix 082
Rich 202
Rich, Matthius 345
Richardson 073
Richardson, Wm. 256
Ridding 245
Ritter, Hannah 165
Ritter, Moses 165
Roberds, Wm. 345
Roberts, Richard 311
Robeson, John 345
Rodman, Wm. W. 169
de Romanzoff, Nicholas 177
Rowe, Larkins 239
Ruggles 073
Ruggles, Alexander 169
Ruggles, N. W. 345
Russ, Joseh 169
Russ, Sempronius 169
Russ, Thomas 169, 345

Sampson, Henry 345
Sampson, John 292

Sampson, Mary Ann 317
Sampson, Michael 119, 317
Sampson, William 119
Saunders, Samuel 153
Saurie 104
Scott, John 345
Scott, Joseph 171
Scott, R. 345
Scull, Maj. John G. 169, 345
Sears, Richard 169
Sebastiani, Gen. 204
Selby, William 169
Shaw 245
Sidbury, Stockley 321
Siddon, Mrs. 137
Sikes 289 (2), 318
Simpson, Tabitha 345
Sinclair, Lieut. Arthur 335
Smith 183, 224, 303, 318
Smith, Benjamin 009, *footnote* 8 (page 6), 048, 049, 167, 184, 228
Smith, David 173
Smith, Capt. H. 345
Smith, James 214, 345
Smith, John 169, 345
Smith, Thomas 068, 085
Smith, William 169
Smollett, Tobias G. 293
Snead, Thomas 345
Southerland, Wm. 082
Spendlove, Jenriet 169
Stanley, Jonathan 345
Starr 336
Starr, Clement 112
Stokes, Montford 160
Stopford, Admiral 201
Story, Mr. 050
Sullivan, Bryant 262
Sullivan, Lydia 345
Sutton 012
Sutton, Ephraim 169
Swain 183
Swaine, Z. 110, 345
Swann, John 169
Swann, Sam'l 169
Sweney, Thomas 169
Swift, L. M. 345

Tarbe, Mr. 091
Tatem, Capt. 180
Taylor, Capt. 274
Taylor, John 345
Telfair, James 262
Thally, Andrew 248
Thomas, John 086 (2)
Thomas, Mr. John 166
Thompson 245, 318
Tom, runaway 264
Treadwell, Gov. John
Trippe 318 (2)
Troup, Mr. 098
Trumbell, Gov. Jonathan 332

75

Truxton, Comm. 076
Tucker 245 (2)
Tuman, David 345
Turner, William L. 343
Twitty, Allen 240

Usher, Ann Eliza *footnote* 18 (page 19)
Usher, James 019, 339
Usher, John 019, 150

Van, Wm. H. 345
VanCortlandt, Mr. 050
Vaughan, James 169
Veragan, Madame 345

Waddle, John 345
Waddle, Moses 169
Wadham 104, 202, 224, 289, 303
Walker, Capt. 159
Walker, Carleton 192, 345
Walker, David 169
Walker, Margaret 345
Wallace, Christopher 169, 345
Ward, Col. 187
Ward, Edward 169, 213
Warner 245 (2)
Warton 012
Warton, Chloe 169
Washington 097
Waters, Elizabeth 169
Watson 104, *footnote* 31 (page 46)
Watson, John A. 345
Watson, Thomas (page 1), 021, 024, 034, 036,
    footnote 18 (page 19), 090, 096, 223, 325,
    347, 348
Watterman, Eleazer 345
Watters, Henry 345
Webb, Capt. 268
Wellman 224, 318
West 012
Wharffs, Barney 170
Wharton, Robert 076
Wheaton 202, 224
Wheeler, Amos 346

Whitby 164, 289 (2), 318
White 224, 245
White, Enrique *footnote* 29 (page 34)
White, James 040
White, Joseph 169
Whitemarsh 318
Whitesides, Capt. 243
Wicker, Joseph 169
Wiley, Thos. 345
Wilkes, Wm. 345
Wilkings, John 169, 345
Wilkins, Capt. *footnote* 17 (page 18)
Wilkinson, Benjamin 219
Wilkinson, Gen. James 091, 287, 309
Wilkinson, Joseph 095, 219
Wilkinson, Thomas B. 169
Wilkinson, Wm. 169
Will, runaway 139
Williams, Capt. 299
Williams, John 249, 280
Williams, Lott 169
Williams, Robert 095, 345
Williams, Wm. 345
Willkings, Wm. A. 144, 345
Wilson 224 (2), 289 (2)
Wilson, Mares 169
Wingate, Mr. 091
Wingate, William 172
Winkoy 088
Winslow, Mr. E. 278
Wisbee, James R. 169
Woistwick, John 169
Wood 245
Wood, Eluathan 169
Wood, Jonathan 169
Wright, Daniel 156
Wright, Joshua Grainger 008 (2)
Wright, Robert 242, 301
Wright, Thomas 121, 169, 256

Yorkshire, runaway 311
Young, Henry 264
Younger, Miss 169

The True Republican or American Whig 1809
By Joseph E. Waters Sheppard

SUBJECTS INDEX

Academy, Harmonic Society 189, 275
The Adventures of Roderick Random 293
Africa or African 091, *footnote* 20 (page 22), 139, 206
Age of Sail *footnote* 5 (page 4), *footnote* 7 (page 5)
Agent for the State 009
Agricultural advice 226, 250, 310
Ale house 037
Almanac for 1809 021
Amelia Island, Florida 098, 161, 164, 183
American Antiquarian Society (page 2)
American Revolutionary War. *See* Wars
Andalusia, Spain 178
Anglo-mania 051
Animals or livestock 114, 203, 286; Horses 072, 086, 114, 144, 172, 187, 311, 338; pad 227
Antigua 303
Apprentices. *See* Occupations, Apprentice
Army 048, 049, 055, 091, 211, 222, 228
Artilleries 175
Attorney for the United States 192, 240
Attorneys or lawyers. *See* Occupations, Attorneys
Auctions 066, 067, 110, 194, 245, 306, 307
Augusta, Georgia 331
Aurora, Philadelphia 076, 108
Austria 287, 297, 335

Bacon 015, 046, 081, 148
Bake-house 115, 193
Baking business 193
Baltimore, Maryland 246
Baltimore Evening Post 027, 288
Bank of Cape Fear 007, 008, 018, 033, 040, 246, 282
Barbados 166, 183
Barrel staves. *See* Staves
Bay of Biscay 330
Bay River, North Carolina 291
Beaufort, North Carolina 245
Beaufort County, North Carolina 167
Beef 046, 054, 148, 236, 285; steer 286
Beer 283
Beeswax 046, 148
Belvedere 167, 184, 228
Bengal 203
Berlin Decree *footnote* 21 (page 22), 105
Bermuda 064, 182
Beverly, Massachusetts 245, 289
Birds 203
Bladen County, North Carolina 345
Board of Commissioners 017
Boats and ships. *See* Ships and boats
Books or bookseller (page 1), *footnote* 9 (page 7), 034, 035, 116, 120, 252, 266, 275, 277, 290, 293, 342
Bordeaux 038, 041
Boston, Massachusetts 012, 045, 053, 065, 073, 077, 104, 166, 180, 183, 202, 245, 246, 289, 299, 318, 334, 336
Boston Centinel 105

Boston Chronicle 229
Boston Detector 053
Boston Patriot 225
Boston Repertory 267
Boundary line with South Carolina 160
Brandy 046, 148, 282
Brazil or Brazilian 071, *footnote* 17 (page 18), 209
Bricks, brick laying business or brick houses 017, 020, 255, 259, 262
Brig Alexis 012
Brig America 245
Brig Catharine 202
Brig Claris 303
Brig Clarisa 164
Brig Equator 245, 318
Brig Fortitude 289
Brig George 041
Brig Hornet 198
Brig Iris 303, 318
Brig Joseph 334
Brig Joshua Potts 336
Brig Julian 299
Brig Nautilus 335
Brig Neptune 336
Brig Paul Hamilton 164
Brig Portland 012
Brig Reliance 073
Brig Sally 289
Brig Sterling 318
Brig Virginia 073
Brigades 049, 167
Brigantine *footnote* 5 (page 5)
Bristol, England 041
British or English *footnote* 2 (page 3), 010, 027, *footnote* 13 (page 10), 042, *footnote* 14 (page 11), 051, 054, 060, 061, 064, *footnote* 17 (page 18), 076, *footnote* 21 (page 22), *footnote* 25 (page 27), 151, 159, 180, 198, 200, 201, 209, 229, 235, 270, 287, 316
British America 201
British Secretary of State 060
Brunswick, Germany 041
Brunswick County, North Carolina 085, 139, 172, 184, 194, 228, 263, 321, 345
Burgos, Spain 204
Burgwin & Orme 168, 253
Butter 046, 148, 236

Cabinetmaker 033
Cadiz, Spain 054, 157, 178, 191, 299
Caicos Islands *footnote* 25 (page 27)
Calicoes 174
Canada *footnote* 25 (page 27), 201
Cannibalism 292
Cannons *footnote* 7 (page 5)
Cape Fear Notes 040
Cape Fear River 192
Captains, of army or ship. *See* Occupations, captains
Capuchins 191
Caribbean *footnote* 25 (page 27)

77

Carlstadt, Sweden 232
Carteret County, North Carolina 167, 184, 228
Carthage, Africa 206
Cash. *See* Money
Cashier 007
Cattle 114
Cedar Grove, North Carolina 244
Cemeteries,
    Bellefontaine Cemetery, St. Louis *footnote* 31 (page 46)
    Christ Church in Boston 166
    Cross Creek Cemetery, Cumberland County *footnote* 33 (page 50)
    Oak Hill, Washington, DC *footnote* 14 (page 11)
    St. James, Wilmington *footnote* 4 (page 4), *footnote* 12 (page 9)
    St. Martin-in-the-Fields 293
    Smithville, North Carolina *footnote* 16 (page 17)
Charleston, Maryland *footnote* 14 (page 11)
Charleston, South Carolina 012, 038, 045, 073, 086, 088, 104, 152, 164, 183, 198, 202, 245, 289, 303, 318, 336
Chatham County Courthouse 258
China 221
Chocolate 174
Cincinnatus of America 150
Codfish 174
Coffee 015, 046, 076, 115, 135, 148, 174, 199, 202, 245
Collector's Office, Port of Wilmington 057, 192; of Boston 065, 077; of New York 330
Columbia River 219
Commander-in-Chief 009
Commercial Treaty 209
Commissioners of North Carolina 160
Commissioners of Wilmington 193
Committee of Commerce 050
Congress 003, *footnote* 1 (page3), 028, 042, 050, 060, 087, 091, 102, 298, 312
Connecticut (page 1), 026, *footnote* 12 (page 9), 153, 332
Continental Line 4th NC *footnote* 18 (page 19)
Copenhagen 328
Cork, Ireland 064
Corn 015, 046, 114, 148, 172, 187
Cotton 040, 070, 098, 148, 192, 278, 282; agricultural 250
Council of Prizes, Paris 208
Counting house 257
Court or courts,
    District of Cape Fear 066, 067, 084, 192; of Pleas & Quarter Sessions *footnote* 10 (page 7); of North Carolina 217
Courthouse in Smithville, North Carolina 017
Courthouse in Wilmington 017, 091, 192, 211
Craven County, North Carolina 167, 184, *footnote* 31 (page 46), 228, 291
Creole 086

Crime, Assault 237; Counterfeiting 240; Forgery 082; Murder 055, 094, 109, 181; Smuggling 098; Theft 086, 142
Cuba 245, 315
Cumberland County *footnote* 36 (page 67), 345
Cypress 046
Cyrene 208

Death notices,
    Alston *footnote* 22 (page 23)
    Beck 133
    Berry *footnote* 26 (page 28)
    Bradey *footnote* 28 (page 29)
    Conway 181
    Dickson 047
    Gillett, *footnote* 12 (page 9)
    Hall, E. 132
    Hall, S. *footnote* 9 (page 7)
    Harrington 162
    Hasell, *footnote* 10 (page 7)
    Hewson 293
    Jones 147
    Madison 163
    Malbourne 302
    Monnino 186
    Muter 011
    Ramsey 349
    Thomas 166
    White *footnote* 29 (page 34)
Democratic Party (page 1), 108
Denmark 328
Derna, Tripoli *footnote* 20 (page 22)
Deserters 013, 175
Desertion, spouse 165
Directors of the Bank of Cape Fear 007, 008
District Court of Cape Fear. *See* Court
Distressed seamen 038, 050
Division of the Militia of NC 049, 184, 228
Dock Street 115, 341
Doctor or physician. *See* Occupations, Doctor
Downs, English Channel *footnote* 17 (page 18)
Duck 174
Duels or dueling 055
Dundee, Scotland 047
Duplin County, North Carolina 069, 082, 087, 103, 114, 133, 154, 167, 248
Durham County, North Carolina 292
Dutch *footnote* 6 (page 5)

Early National Era (page 1)
East Indies 219
Edenton, North Carolina 129
Editors. *See* Occupations, Editors
Effex Junta 070, 159
Elections (page 1), 052, 054, 083, 091
Embargo of 1807 *footnote* 2 (page 3), 002, 026, 041, 043, 050, 057, 063, 070, 092, 098, 102, 108, 128, 155, 157, 210
Embargo Act *footnote* 2 (page 3); Bill for enforcing 003, 057, 070; Repeal 001, 059
Encyclopedia Perthensis 190

England *footnote* 14 (page 11), 041, 051, 064, 070, 151, 177, 182, 225, 235, 260, 288, 299
English. *See* British
English hunting gun 212
Erfurth 177
Erin 108, 149
Esquires. *See* Occupations, Esquire
Essex *footnote* 21 (page 22)
Estate sales 114, 147
Ewan's Alley 123
Exuma 088

Fairfield Plantation 132
Falmouth, England 064, 159, 200
Fayetteville, North Carolina 079, 171, *footnote* 33 (page 50), 258
Fayetteville Academy 343
Fayetteville Observer footnote 9 (page 7)
Federal Court for North Carolina 217, 240, 329
Federalist 065, 072, 158, 210, 300
1st Regiment U. S. Artilleries 175
First Street 018, 033
Fishing *footnote* 25 (page 27), 261
Flax 040, 046, 148, 192
Florida *footnote* 14 (page 11), 098, 161, 186
Flour 015, 046, 054, 148, 236, 268, 283, 285
Forgery 082
Fort Johnston *footnote* 16 (page 17)
Fowling 261
France 027, 041, 053, *footnote* 17 (page 18), 105, 157, 177, 204, 233, 270, 288
Franklin County, North Carolina 094
French *footnote* 2 (page 3), 041, *footnote* 21 (page 22), 105, 130, 151, 178, 179, 199, 200, 205, 208, 218, 221, 231, 287, 299, 315
French language 176, 195, 212, 341
French's Neck 311
Frigate 182
Front Street 120, 123, 255

Ganges River 203
Gautier & co. 032, 039, 236
General Assembly 147, 237, 308
General Assembly of Connecticut 332
Gentlemen. *See* Occupations, gentlemen
Georgetown, D. C. *footnote* 14 (page 11), 219
Georgia 086, 098, 250, 331
Germans or Germany 030, *footnote* 11 (page 8), 157, 287
Giles & Burgwin 031
Gilkings Creek, South Carolina 118
Gin 046, 148, 174, 282, 285
Gloucester, Massachusetts 045, 245
Goshen, North Carolina 069
Governor of Connecticut 332
Governor of Florida 161
Governor of Maryland 242, 301
Governor of Mississippi 095
Governor of North Carolina 091
Governor of Virginia *footnote* 1 (page 3)
Granville County, North Carolina 094
Graves. *See* Cemeteries

Great Britain 041, 063, 098, 105, 210
Great Cumberland Place 061, 063
Greene County, North Carolina 184, 228
Greenland 138
Grenada 336
Grenada, Spain 178
Guadeloupe Island 041, 233
Gun, English hunting 212
Gunboats. *See* Ships and boats
Gunpowder 236

Halifax 220
Halifax County, North Carolina 094
Hall & Nichols 322
Ham 015
Hardware & ship chandlery 173
Harmonic Society 189
Harwick 289
Havana, Cuba 164, 179, 199, 218, 245
Health, ailments *footnote* 9 (page 7), 284, 341
Heaven 051, 132
The Herald. See Newbern Herald
The History of the United States, 1801 to 1809 252
Hogs 114
Holland 299
Horse or horses. *See* Animals
Hotels 018, 080
House of Representatives 004, 028, 050, 060, 065, 098, 107, 155, 298, 312
House servants 044
Houses or buildings for rent 019, 116, 117, 122, 123, 255
Houses or buildings for sale 069, 080, 114, 122, 164, 337
Hyde County, North Carolina 167

Illinois 243
Impeachment 065, 072
Indian Creek, North Carolina 140
Indian war 242
Indiana 109
Inspection returns 049
Insurrection. *See* Wars
Ireland or Irish (page 1), 064, 138, 149, 150, 206, 236
Iron 196, 283, 285
Italy or Italian 206, 208

Jail 118, 139, 140, 170, 171, 175, 181, 213, 247, 264, 339
Jamaica 011, 092, 148, 315, 318
Jeffersonian Republicans (page 1)
Johnston County, North Carolina 184, 228
Jon carpenters 014
Jones County, North Carolina 213
Judges. *See* Occupations, Judges
Jury or juries 055

Kaskaskia, Indiana 109
Kent, Ireland 206
King of Holland 234
King of Sweden 232, 235
Kingston, Jamaica 092, 318

Lancaster, Pennsylvania 023
Land for sale 069, 214
Lard 015, 046
Latin grammar 176, 284
Leesburg, Virginia 055
Lenoir County, North Carolina 184, 228
Leonidas 131
Lessingwell, England 064
Letter or letters,
    by a gentleman in Marblehead 070
    communication from Pres. Adams 225
    Corbett's letter to the king 327
    extract from Savannah 161
    extract of a letter from Havana 179
    extracts read by Mr. Troup 098
    from Paris about Emperor of China 221
    from a Gentleman at Liverpool 002
    from Havana 199
    from a respectable house in Kingston 092
    list in the Post Office 169, 345
    of President Adams 156
    of Mr. Canning and British 060, 061, 062, 063
    of the parents, expressing satisfaction 341
    Sir John Moore's, House of Commons 296
Library 277
Lisbon, Portugal *footnote* 17 (page 18), 157, 174, 281, 299
List of Letters 169, 345
Liverpool, England 002, 012, 026, 046, 064, 104, 148, 201, 303
Livery stables 144
Livestock See Animals
Lloyd & Anderson 342
London, England 060, 062, 157, 159, 195, 200, 209, 231, 281, 287, 296, 323
Long Creek, North Carolina 171
Lost money 040
Lottery 121
Loudon County, Virginia 055
Louisburg 219
Louisiana 243
Lower Elbe 235
Lugger Alarm *footnote* 17 (page 18)
Lugger Fair Trader 067, *footnote* 15 (page 17)
Lumber 015, 046, 113, 148, 237

McNeill & Co. 014
Madrid, Spain 281
Magistrate of Police 193
Malaga 334
Malanzas 202
Mandarins 221
Mantanzas 012
Marblehead, Massachusetts 070
Marietta, Ohio 230
Marine Invalid Case 208
Marine list. *See* Port of Wilmington
Market Street. *See* Wilmington streets
Marriage notices,
    Campbell and Mallett 079
    Cooke and Buxton 154
    Gibson and Creighton 010
    Hill and Dudley 103
    Holmes and Norman 154
    Jocelyn and Sampson 317
    Kenan and James 154
    M'Lin and Beitner 154
    Mabson and Moore 244
    Saunders and Bailard 153
    Watson and Hannis 223
Martinique 220, 233
Maryland 042, *footnote* 14 (page 11), 095, 219, 301
Massachusetts 070, 073, 075, 106, 156, 158, 166, 289
MENTOR 056, 074, 078, 089, 100, 210, 260, 270
Merchant ships 225
Merchants. *See* Occupations, merchants
Military & Naval affairs 029
Militia 009, 093, 211
Mississippi 095, 243
Missouri (pages 1-2), 219, *footnote* 31 (page 46)
Mogul 203
Molasses 015, 046, 148, 174, 245
Mold 187
Money, bonds, notes or cash 040, 064, 085, 086, 096, 109, 111, 121, 140, 141, 168, 171, 172, 175, 187, 188, 189, 190, 199, 212, 213, 215, 237, 240, 246, 247, 343, 346, 347
Mulattos 118, 179, 258, 262
Murder 055, 094, 109, 181
Music 032, 034, 091, 143, Harmonic Society 189, 275, 341
Muster rolls 049

Nankeens 253, 282
Nantucket 289, 303
Napoleonic Wars. *See* Wars
Natchez, Tennessee *footnote* 31 (page 46), 331
National Intelligence/r. *See* Newspapers
Naval Service, U.S. 013, 050
Naval stores 046, 098, 148, 279
Negroes 044, 085, 127, 139, 140, 142, 171, 179, 213, 247, 248, 263, 264, 280, 291, 321, 339, 348; child in deed *footnote* 18 (page 19)
New Bern, NC, (page 1), 012, *footnote* 9 (page 7), 069, 154, 213, 311
New Bern Weekly Advertiser (page 1)
New England 158
New Hanover County, North Carolina *footnote* 10 (page 7), 228, 345
New Hanover County Militia 211
New Jersey 187
New London 041
New Orleans, Louisiana 009, 086, *footnote* 31 (page 46), 287, 309, 315
New Portugal 209
New-River, North Carolina 088, 164, 183, 289, 311, 318
New York 012, 041, 054, 064, 073, 158, 159, 178, 183, 195, 199, 200, 202, 245, 246, 287, 289, 299, 303, 313, 318, 336, 341, 342
New York State Lottery 121
Newark, New Jersey 187
Newbern, NC. *See* New Bern, NC

Newbern Herald (page 1), 036, 223
Newport 303, 318
Newspapers,
    Aurora, Philadelphia 076
    Baltimore Evening Post 027, 288
    Bell's Messenger, London 323
    Boston Centinel 105
    Boston Chronicle 229
    Boston Detector 053
    Boston Patriot 225
    Boston Repertory 267
    City Gazette, Charleston, SC 152
    Enquirer, Philadelphia 158
    Fayetteville Observer footnote 9 (page 7)
    Mercantile Advertiser 179
    National Intelligence/r, Washington 097, 159, 219, 299, 302, 326
    New Bern Weekly Advertiser (page 1)
    Newbern Herald (page 1), 036, 223
    Petersburg Rep. 072
    Raleigh Minerva 240, 272
    Raleigh Register 160, 349
    Salem Register 043
    Seville Gazette, Spain 186
    Staunton Eagle, Virginia 055
    The True Republican, New Bern (page 1)
    The True Republican, Wilmington (pages 1-2), 005, 006, 024, 036, 074, 089, 090, 096, 099, 100, 101, 197, 223, 290, 347
    Vincennes newspaper, Indiana 243
    Washington Monitor 041, 059, 108, 260
    Wilmington Advertiser footnote 12 (page 9)
    Wilmington Gazette (pages 1-2), 024, 051, *footnote* 17 (page 18), 082, 089, 101, 145, 151, 300
    Wilmington Weekly Chronicle footnote 9 (page 7)
Non-Intercourse Act *footnote* 2 (page3), 102
Norfolk, Virginia 159, 268
North Carolina District Court 217
North Salem, Massachusetts 043
North Sea 323
Northampton, Massachusetts 156
Northern Confederacy 158
Northeast River, North Carolina 171, 214, 311
Northwest River, North Carolina 140
Norway 136, 166, *footnote* 32 (page 48), 328
Nova Scotia 201

Occupations or titles,
    Admiral 182, 201
    Agent for the State 009
    Aid de' camp 048
    Ambassador 177, 205, 209, 251
    Apprentices 099, 170, 188, 215, 239, 304
    Artist for the state 272
    Astronomer 160
    Attorneys or lawyers 032, 039, 076, 081, 192, 237, 240, 319
    Bank directors 007, 008
    Bank president 008
    Bookseller (page 1), *footnote* 9 (page 7)
    Brigadier General 331
    Cabinetmaker 033
    Captain, army 175
    Captains of ships 010, 038, 041, *footnote* 13 (page 10), *footnote* 17 (page 18), 091, 110, 152, 161, 178, 180, 198, 213, 268, 334
    Carpenter 292
    Carriage maker 175
    Cashier 007
    Chief Justice 240
    Clergyman 081, 136
    Clerk, superior court 345
    Clerk, town 058, 194
    Collector, Port of Wilmington 057, 192; of Boston 065, 077; of N. York 330
    Colonel 187, 211
    Commander-in-Chief 009
    Commissioners 017, 058, 160, 193, 272, 320
    Commodore 091
    Consul, American 071
    Count 177, 186
    Customer 080
    Deputy marshal 066, 067
    Devil 081
    Doctor or physician 055, 068, *footnote* 16 (page 17), *footnote* 18 (page 19), 109, 160, 293, 344
    Duchess 234
    Duke 204, 234, 287
    Duke of York 271
    Editors (page 1), 005, 006, 041, 051, 101, 179, 197, 222, 223, 225, 295, 300, 309
    Emperor 041, 157, 177, 221, 234, 297
    Esquires 048, 053, 079, 091, 109, 143, 156, 192, 257, 261, 301, 302, 317
    Field Marshal 191
    Generals *footnote* 17 (page 18), 091, 105, 160, 162, 219
    Gentlemen 002, 008, 033, 037, 041, 054, 070, 072, 081, 098, 105, 144, 159, 176, 185, 195, 212, 219, 227, 308
    Governor *footnote* 1 (page 3), 023, 091, 095, 158, 161, 242, 301, 315
    Hairdresser 293
    House servants 044
    Hunters 219
    Inspector of Naval Stores 279
    Jon carpenters 014
    Judges 108, 192, 240
    Jurist 055
    Kings 040, *footnote* 17 (page 18), 191, 225, 232, 234, 235
    Lieutenant 055, *footnote* 20 (page 22), 222, 335
    Lieut. General 296
    Lieut. Governor 075
    Major 048, 211, 345
    Major General 009, 048, 049, 167, 184, 228

Marines *footnote* 20 (page 22)
Marshall 240
Masters of vessels 262, 263, 264, 291, 292, 321
Mayor, Philadelphia 076
Merchants 011, 026, 034, 035, 070, 092, 154, 181, 305, 317
Militia 009
Minister of religion 169, 191, 343
Minister of state 038, 060, 159, 177, 233
Overseer 265
Passenger 064, 178, 315
Peasants 231
Physician. *See* Occupations, Doctor
Planter *footnote* 28 (page 29), 158, 226, 250, 305
Police 193
Postmaster (page 1)
President (page 1), 052, 083, 091, 102, 107, 151, 156, 163, 225, 241, 288
Priest 191
Prince regent Portugal 071, *footnote* 17 (page 18); Princes of Rhinnish 205; Prince of Lucca 234
Princess 234
Printers 347
Prisoner 204
Queen *footnote* 17 (page 18)
Rector 030, 079
Relict 011
Representative 004
Sailors 076, 213, 292
Seamen 038, 050, 210, 225, 316
Seamstress 280
Secretary for the Dept. of War 241
Secretary of state 159, 177
Senator 001, 003, *footnote* 1 (page 3), 298, 302
Sheriff 154, 169, 276, 345
Silversmith 304
Squire 227
Statesman *footnote* 1 (page 3)
Tailor 340
Teachers 034, 143, 176, 212, 284, 341, 343, 346
Trappers 219
Treasurer, county 276
Trustees, school 343
Vice-president 052, 091
Viscount 296
Warriors 219
Watchmaker 185
Wife 165, 171, 213, 227, 264, 311, 321
Ohio 230
Old Town Plantation *footnote* 26 (page 28)
Onslow County, North Carolina 103, 167, 184, 311
Oporto 053
Orange County, Virginia 163
Orange Street 117, 195, 212
Orders in Council *footnote* 21 (page 22)
Outhouses 069
Oxen 114

Packer Princess Amelia Morson 064
Packet 038, *footnote* 13 (page 10), 068, 159
Packet Carteret, British 200
Paradise Lost footnote 11 (page 8)
Paris, France 177, 208, 234
Peas 015, 046, 148
Pennsylvania 023, 108
Persia 251
Petersburg Rep. 072
Philadelphia, Pennsylvania 002, 006, 012, 016, 076, 088, 158, 182, 196, 197, 202, 236, 245, 246, 274, 278, 294, 314, 318, 328, 336
Physicians. *See* Occupations, Doctors
Pistols 055, 094
Pitt County, North Carolina 184, 228
Plantations or farms 069, 140,
    Ashe Plantation, Rocky Point 247
    Belvedere 167, 184, 228
    Fairfield Plantation 132
    Hilton 261
    Moore plantation 259
    Old Town Plantation *footnote* 26 (page 28)
    Sloop Point 311
Plymouth, North Carolina 202
Pork 015, 054, 148, 285
Port of Wilmington, entered and cleared 012, 045, 057, 073, 088, 104, 164, 183, 192, 245, 289, 303, 318, 336. *See also* Ships and boats
Portsmouth, New Hampshire 245, 289, 303
Portsmouth, Virginia *footnote* 4 (page 4)
Portugal 071, *footnote* 17 (page 18), 157, 209
Post Office *footnote* 13 (page 10), 087, 169, 345
Potatoes 236
Presbyterian Church *footnote* 33 (page 50), *footnote* 36 (page 67)
Presidents of the United States (page 1), 003, 060, 065, 072, 091, 101, 151, 156, 225, 241, 252, 288
Prices Current 015, 148
Prison and stocks 194
Privateer L'Eve 208
Providence, Rhode Island 045, 073, 245, 289
Puans 243
Public auctions. *See* Auctions
Public toasts 131, 149, 230

Quincy, Massachusetts 156, 225

Raleigh, North Carolina 087, 160, 171, 181, 217, 329,
Raleigh Academy 343
Raleigh Minerva 240, 272
Raleigh Register 160
Ravens duck 174
Rebellion Roads, Charleston 198
Rector 030, 079
Republican Party (page 1), 027, 043, 051, 151, 156, 210, 269, 300
Revolution of 1800 (page 1)
Revolutionary War. *See* Wars, American
Rhinnish Confederacy 205
Rhode Island 013, 298, 302

Rice 015, 040, 046, 113, 148, 192, 261, 265, 305;
    agricultural 226
Richmond County, North Carolina 162
Right Honorable Benefit 137
Rio Janeiro, Brazil 073, 209
Rocky Point, North Carolina 247, 311
Roman Catholic 221. *See also* Capuchins
Rome or Romans 206, 281
Rum 015, 046, 148, 274, 282, 285
Runaway apprentices 170, 188, 215, 239
Runaway slaves 085, 118, 127, 139, 140, 171, 213,
    247, 248, 258, 262, 263, 264, 280, 291, 311,
    321, 339
Russia or Russian 041, 174, 177, 287, 297

Saint Augustine, Florida 161
St. Bartholomew Island 164, 183, 268, 289, 315
St. Christopher's 323
St. Croix Island 180, 213
St. Domingo 086, 180
St. Jago, Cuba 245, 315
St. James Cemetery. *See* Cemeteries
St. James Church, Wilmington 030, *footnote* 18 (page 19)
St. Louis, Missouri (pages 1-2), 219, *footnote* 31 (page 46)
St. Louis Missouri Company 219
St. Lucar 054
St. Lucia 041
St. Mary's, Georgia 086
St. Mary's River, Florida 098
St. Patrick's Day 149
St. Petersburgh 281
St. Salvador 071
St. Simon, Georgia 250
Salem, Massachusetts 073, 245, 318
Salem Register 043
Salt 015, 028, 046, 124, 129, 148, 174
Sampson County, North Carolina 093, 154, 171, 317
Saragossa, Spain 200, 207
Savannah, Georgia 175
Schools or school house 034, 194, 341, 343, 346
Schooner Abigail 245, 289
Schooner Adams 336
Schooner Amanda 073, 183, 313, 318
Schooner Ann Eliza 073
Schooner Anne 073
Schooner Aurora 164
Schooner Azubah & Ruthy 245
Schooner Betsy 202, 289
Schooner Betty 012
Schooner Buonaparte 303
Schooner Catharine 202
Schooner Catharine Shepherd 268
Schooner Charlotte 303
Schooner Comet 183, 202, 289
Schooner Corotoman 274
Schooner Delesdemier 245
Schooner Dolphin 010, 307
Schooner Dover 318
Schooner Eagle 164, 289, 318
Schooner Enterprize 012, 202

Schooner Gulielma 202
Schooner Harmony 073, 104, 278, 318
Schooner Harriet 289
Schooner Heart-of-Oak 289, 303
Schooner Henry Dennison 012
Schooner Isabella 012, 202, 222, 306
Schooner Jane 053
Schooner Jefferson 318
Schooner Julia & Sally 336
Schooner Little John 183, 289, 318
Schooner Maria 202 (2)
Schooner Mercury 245
Schooner Milly 289
Schooner Nancy 289
Schooner P. D. Experiment 183
Schooner Patty 073, 245
Schooner Polly 164, 183, 245, 289, 303
Schooner President 318
Schooner Prudentia 245
Schooner R. Prosperis 183
Schooner Rebecca 012, 183
Schooner Regulator 073, 104, 164, 202, 245, 289, 303
Schooner Resolution 183, 318
Schooner Return 073, 289, 318
Schooner Revenge 183
Schooner Richard 218
Schooner Rising Sun 318, 336
Schooner Rover 164, 289
Schooner Ruby 245
Schooner Sally 336
Schooner Sally & Betty 183
Schooner Scythian 245, 289
Schooner Sea Horse 202
Schooner Sunbury 318
Schooner Telegraph 068, 164
Schooner Temperance 318
Schooner Theoda 066
Schooner Three Brothers 336
Schooner Three Sisters 183
Schooner Traveler 202, 336
Schooner Triall 303
Schooner Trio 012
Schooner Tryall 289
Schooner Vandyck 245
Schooner Venus 073, 120, 202, 289, 303, 342
Scotland 047
Seamen. *See* Occupations, Seamen
Second Street 018, 024, 080, 325
Secretary of State for Foreign Affairs 071, 076
Secretary of the Treasury 004
Senate of the United States 001, 003, 026, 060, 091
Seville, Spain 186
Shallotte, North Carolina 303
Sheep 114
Sheriff of Duplin 154
Sheriff of New Hanover 169, 345
Sheriff of Sampson 154
Ship Acorn 292
Ship Augusta 208
Ship Bedford 303
Ship Charles Carter 202
Ship Cora 170

The True Republican or American Whig 1809
By Joseph E. Waters Sheppard

Ship Eliza Ann 299
Ship Flora 315
Ship Herkimer 287
Ship Mary 012
Ship Monticello 292
Ship Ophelia 041
Ship Perseverance 110, 164, 183
Ship Philipsburgh 064
Ship Rover 246
Ship Snow Fanny 289
Ship Thomas Jefferson 178
Ship Virginia 316
Ships and boats,
    Brigantine *footnote* 5 (page 5)
    Brigs 012, *footnote* 5 (page 4), 045, 073, 104, 164, 198, 201, 202, 245, 289, 299, 318, 334
    Cruisers *footnote* 17 (page 18)
    Frigate 182
    Gunboats 003, 013, *footnote* 7 (page 5), 091, 098, 101, 216
    Lugger 067, *footnote* 15 (page 17), *footnote* 17 (page 18)
    Merchant vessels 299
    Packer 064
    Packet 038, *footnote* 13 (page 10), 068, 159
    Privateer 208
    Schooners 010, 012, *footnote* 3 (page 4), 045, 053, 066, 068, 088, 104, 164, 183, 202, 218, 222, 245, 268, 289, 315, 318
    Sloops 012, *footnote* 6 (page 5), 045, 076, 088, 159, 164, 198, 202, 245, 289, 299, 315, 318
    Vessels 003, 016, 057, 064, 071, 098, 157, 159, 161, 170, 171, 182, 198, 199, 213, 323, 328; Susan 208
    War 003, 064, 076, 159, 198, 299
    Wrecked 274, 292
Ships for sale 110, 246, 306
Ships of war 003, *Lavinia* 064, 159
Shipwrecks 274, 292
Silver spoon, found 259
Slave trade *footnote* 23 (page 24), *footnote* 27 (page 29); child in deed *footnote* 18 (page 19)
Slaves in baking business 193
Slaves, runaway. *See* Runaway slaves
Sloop Betsy 303, 318
Sloop Charlotte 303
Sloop Columbia 245, 303, 318
Sloop Francesco de Pawlo 164
Sloop Friendship *footnote* 6 (page 5)
Sloop George 045, 073
Sloop Hunter 289
Sloop Morning Star 202, 283, 289
Sloop Patty 073, 245
Sloop Patty and Lydia 012, 045
Sloop Point plantation 311
Sloop Rosamond 159
Sloop Rover 318
Sloop-of-War Enterprize 299

Smithville, North Carolina 017, *footnote* 8 (page 6), 068, *footnote* 16 (page 17), 194, 320
Smuggling 098
Soap 174
South America 310
South Carolina 160, 226, 272
South Washington, North Carolina 214
Southport, North Carolina. *See* Smithville
Spain or Spaniards or Spanish 041, 053, 064, *footnote* 17 (page 18), 157, 159, 178, 180, 186, 199, 200, 231, 287, 299, 323, 330
Speech or speeches,
    Mr. Giles' 001
    Mr. Goodrich 003
    Mr. Jackson 155
    Mr. Pickering 059
Spouse desertion 165
Spread Eagle 018
Stables 144
Staunton Eagle, Virginia 055
Staves 015, 046, 066, 113, 148, 168, 174
Steamboat *footnote* 5 (page 5)
Stockholm, Sweden 232
Stone 017
Sugar 015, 046, 115, 148, 174, 199, 202, 245, 285
Surinam 054
Swansboro, North Carolina 183, 289, 303, 318
Sweden or Swedish 202, 222, 232, 235, 287, 328
Swords 254

Tailoring business 188
Tar 015, 046, 054, 148
Tavern 222
Teheran 251
Tennessee 041, 333
Theft 086, 142
Timber 046, 098, 113, 273
Toasting or public toasts 131, 149, 230
Tobacco 015, 040, 046, 070, 148, 174, 285
Toledo, Spain 200
Topsail Sound, North Carolina 104, 164, 274
Toryism 097
Town Creek, North Carolina 263, 264
Trent River, North Carolina 213
Trinidad 104
Tripolitan War 091, *footnote* 20 (page 22)
The True Republican, New Bern (page 1)
The True Republican, Wilmington See Newspapers
Turkey 297
Turks Island 016, 104, 124, *footnote* 25 (page 27), 174
Turpentine 015, 046, 113, 148, 273
Tuscany 234

Uncle Billy footnote 19 (page 20)
Union County, South Carolina 118
Union Street, Charleston 086
Uprisings. *See* Wars

Venice 281
VERITAS 101
Vermont 158

The True Republican or American Whig 1809
By Joseph E. Waters Sheppard

Vessels. *See* Ships and boats
Virginia or Virginian 055, 174, 175, *footnote* 36 (page 67); statesman *footnote* 1 (page 3)

Wales *footnote* 24 (page 26)
Wars or uprising or insurrection,
    American Revolutionary War 042, *footnote* 14 (page 11), *footnote* 18 (page 19), *footnote* 25 (page 27), 162, 315
    Battle of Trafalgar 281
    British forces 271, 287
    Department of War 241
    French ships of war 041
    Guadeloupe 180
    In the Caribbean islands 199, 218, 233, 315
    In Ireland 206
    in Portugal *footnote* 17 (page 18), 157, 299
    in Spain 053, 064, 178, 191, 200, 207, 231, 287, 299
    in Sweden 232, 287
    Indian Wars in Illinois and Louisiana 243
    Napoleonic wars *footnote* 2 (page 3), 040, *footnote* 17 (page 18), 204, 234, 287, 330, 334
    Naval 201, 327
    Tripolitan War 091, *footnote* 20 (page 22)
    United States with Great Britain 070
    West Indies 179
Washington City 038, 106, 146, 159, 219
Washington D. C. *footnote* 14 (page 11)
Washington Monitor 041, 059, 108, 260
Washington, North Carolina 214
Watch making 185, 304
Watson & Ramsey 090, 096, 348
Wayne County, North Carolina 184, 228
Weirmland, Sweden 232
West Indies 041, 179, 182, 233
Whiskey 196, 282, 285
White Marsh 264
Wilmington Advertiser footnote 12 (page 9)
Wilmington, Delaware 045
Wilmington, North Carolina,
    Asylum for runaway slaves 247
    Collector for the Port of 057, 192
    Commissioners of the Town Orders that no straw be kept in any kitchen 058; that baking business is carried on by slaves 193; driving of horses through the streets 338
    Exhibition of the *Wonderful Curiosities* 281
    Houses for rent or sale 019, 069, 080, 114, 116, 117, 122, 123, 255, 337, 344
    Jail 118, 139, 140, 170, 171, 247, 321
    Library 277
    Livery 144
    Newspapers. *See* Newspapers
    Occupations. *See* Occupations
    Port of Wilmington, entered and cleared 012, 045, 057, 073, 104, 164, 183, 202, 245, 289, 303, 318, 336
    Post Office list of letters 169, 345
    Public auctions 066, 067, 110, 194, 246, 306, 307
    Public dinner to celebrate revival of commerce 290
    Public toasts 131, 149
    Recreation and sports, fishing and fowling 261; horseracing 172; reading *See* Books
    Schools 034, 343, 346
Wilmington Gazette. See Newspapers
Wilmington Prices Current 015, 148
Wilmington streets,
    Dock Street 115, 341
    Ewan's Alley 123, 255
    First 018, 033
    Fourth 337
    Front Street 120, 123, 255
    Market 024, *footnote* 16 (page 17), 080, 091, 120, 143, 282, 325, 340
    Orange Street 117, 195, 212, 337
    Second 018, 024, 080, 144, 325
    Third 337
Wilmington Weekly Chronicle footnote 9 (page 7)
Windmill 337
Wine 174, 222, 285
Winnebago 243
Wiscasset 104
Women 010, 011, 044, 079, *footnote* 18 (page 19), 103, 127, 132, 133, 135, 137, 142, 153, 154, 165, 169, 200, 223, 227, 234, 244, 248, 264, 280, 311, 317, 321, 341, 343, 345, 346

ABOUT THE AUTHOR

JOSEPH SHEPPARD, originally from Marietta, Ohio, resides in Wilmington, North Carolina. Since 1996 he has been with the North Carolina Collection of the New Hanover County Public Library, in Wilmington. In addition to his work with the library, he writes feature articles for the Old New Hanover Genealogical Society's *Clarendon Courier*, and was past editor for the Lower Cape Fear Historical Society's *Bulletin*. He teaches family history with the Lifelong Learning Institute of UNC-Wilmington and has been the invited guest lecturer at the North Carolina Genealogical Society's annual meetings. Sheppard is also a favorite guest speaker on North Carolina historical research at numerous historical agencies throughout the state.

www.ingramcontent.com/pod-product-compliance
Lightning Source LLC
Chambersburg PA
CBHW080349170426
43194CB00014B/2730